HANGING IN
AND DROPPING OUT

Voices of At-Risk High School Students

D0024755

HANGING IN AND DROPPING OUT

Voices of At-Risk High School Students

EDWIN FARRELL

Teachers College, Columbia University
New York and London

LA 229
F 36
1990

Published by Teachers College Press, 1234 Amsterdam Avenue
New York, NY 10027

Copyright © 1990 by Teachers College, Columbia University

All rights reserved. No part of this publication may be reproduced
or transmitted in any form or by any means, electronic or mechanical,
including photocopy, or any information storage and retrieval system,
without permission from the publisher.

Library of Congress Cataloging-in-Publication Data

Farrell, Edwin William.
    Hanging in and dropping out: voices of at-risk high school
students / Edwin Farrell.
    p. cm.
    Includes bibliographical references.
    ISBN 0-8077-3004-1 (alk. paper).—ISBN 0-8077-3003-3 (pbk. :
    alk. paper)
    1. High school students—United States—Attitudes. 2. High school
students—United States—Interviews. 3. High schools—United
States. 4. High school dropouts—United States. I. Title.
LA229.F36 1990   89-28620
373.18′1—dc20   CIP

Printed on acid-free paper

Manufactured in the United States of America

96 95 94 93 92 91 90   8 7 6 5 4 3 2 1

To Celia
Who makes all things possible

MY 15 '90

Contents

Acknowledgments

A number of people were instrumental in the process that led to this book. First and foremost, I would like to thank Professor Norman Shapiro of the City College, City University of New York. Norman is a member of my department as well as the director of the Stay-in-School Partnership, a program that links City College with a number of high schools in New York to combat the dropout problem. Without Norman's support this book would not have been possible; I am particularly in his debt because he sought me out to work on various parts of the project. I admire his forbearance at those times when he did not see the value of all of my efforts.

I would like to thank my collaborators on the first part of the project, George Peguero, Rasheed Lindsey, and Ronald White. George, Rasheed, and Ron were students at Louis E. Brandeis High School who interviewed people I never would have been able to.

Julie Espinal, my student at City College, collected data and gave me many valuable insights. She has since become a high school teacher herself.

Madeline Chang and Johanna Young transcribed my data and were absolutely essential to the writing of this book. Madeline is an educator in her own right and Johanna a divinity student. Their comments on the data were always enlightening.

Finally, I thank all my students, past and present, each of whom in some way contributed to this.

HANGING IN AND DROPPING OUT

Voices of At-Risk High School Students

Introduction: The Self at Risk

This is a book about people who are in the wrong place at the wrong time. The words of the book are largely their words. The people are young men and women, 14 to 19 years old. Their assigned place—and for them, the wrong place—is the American high school. Like many others their age they are seeking the answer to the all-important question of their lives, "Where do I fit in?"

The American high school has been able to help large numbers of adolescents, perhaps even the majority, answer this question. But for many it has been ineffective. Unable to find the answers in their assigned place, they do not consider that place to have a great deal of meaning for their lives. Moreover, if remaining in that place adds to their anxieties, they are apt to leave. They become high school dropouts.

The problem of dropping out of school has come to national attention in recent years. The media have addressed it; political figures have bemoaned it; educational researchers have studied it; school practitioners have tried to alleviate it. While there have always been large numbers of people who leave school early, to work or to marry, the problem takes on special significance today because we realize that the need for education increases as the technology of our culture becomes more complex.

To this end, celebrities do TV spots imploring our youth to stay in school. The message that comes across is that students themselves must solve the problem. More effort, more interest, more tenacity, more self-control are the answers. Students are told that the average high school graduate has higher lifetime earnings than the average dropout; the average college graduate has higher lifetime earnings than the average high school graduate. But the statistics of the mythical "average" person may not mean a great deal to someone without a history of success in school and who cannot link quadratic equations, French verbs, and Shakespearean sonnets with the world of work.

1

Critics of education often explain the dropout problem in terms of their own philosophies or social outlooks. Students are oppressed because of their social class or race. Teachers are disempowered. The curriculum is not rigorous enough. Schools are too rigid. Education can do little in light of the genetic makeup of certain groups. But when the dropout rate approaches 50 percent in some places these explanations do not make much sense.

Certainly the middle class gets a bigger piece of the pie, both economically and educationally, and certainly there is racism in our society, but it would hardly be in the best interests of society to oppress that many people. All but the most reactionary elements realize that society functions better as more people become productive contributors. Teachers must have autonomy in what and how they teach, but this in itself does not guarantee more people remaining in school; in order to use whatever autonomy they have, teachers need to know how *students* view their own education.

Conservative critics of education would have us believe that more algebra, more foreign languages, more Shakespeare will improve things. It is hard to believe that any of these critics has ever taught a class of students at risk of dropping out. Liberal critics, on the other hand, argue that students need to have more choice over what they learn, the freedom to make mistakes, and the trust of their elders. Such arguments have validity, but students must also have real responsibilities and these, we shall see, may be even more difficult to acquire than freedom.

That certain students have not experienced academic achievement is obvious, but it strains credibility to say that when 40 percent of students have dropped out of a certain school, they have all done so because of a lack of innate ability. By the time the prospective dropout arrives in high school, she usually has a history of poor academic performance, has not developed a positive attitude toward schoolwork, and may have one or more serious skill deficiencies in the three R's. This might be the result of cultural, socioeconomic, instructional, familial, emotional factors, or even innate ability, but I take it as an article of faith that the vast majority of children start kindergarten with the intellectual wherewithal to complete high school twelve years later.

However, this book is about practical concerns of specific students; a high school is made up of specific students. Teachers and principals cannot just throw up their hands and claim that some proportion of the population will not be able to graduate. You create programs for the students you have. Those who are in the right place at the right time are fortunate, and they are likely to respond to the traditional high school program. The others, up to 50 percent of the population, may need different programs and different places, but the similarities among high school students, I believe, far outweigh the differences. The concept of adolescence that underlies this book is based on those similarities.

THE TASK OF THE ADOLESCENT

Erik Erikson (1963) in his most famous book, *Childhood and Society*, gave the world the concept of ego identity. To Erikson, the ego is a central principle of organization within the individual; it must integrate growth with the structure of social institutions. Identity is that quality of the ego that emerges largely during the critical period of adolescence. The young person has to deal with a physiological revolution inside of him and "tangible adult tasks" ahead of him. He seeks to connect "the roles and skills cultivated earlier with the occupational prototypes of the day" (p. 261).

But Erikson (1963) cautions us that the ego is a principle of organization and not an entity. Therefore I would like to use a more general term, one less identified with psychoanalysis than is ego identity, to describe what happens in adolescence. The adolescent is trying to create a particular sense of *self*. But the self, according to Harry Stack Sullivan (1953), is a system created in our interpersonal relationships. In order to develop this system the adolescent must integrate a number of what might be competing selves. The primary self that the adolescent strives for, if Erikson is correct, can be called "self-as-my-work"; I am a (future) carpenter, lawyer, rock star. Other possible selves are self-in-family, sexual self, self-as-loyal-friend, self-in-peer-group, self-as-student, and for some, self-as-parent.

Self-in-Family. This is the primary self that is deposited at the kindergarten classroom door. For most of us, our families are our major support systems through adolescence and perhaps through the rest of our lives. At adolescence, however, our family can become the source of most of our prohibitions and many of our irritations. It need not, but often does conflict with the following three selves.

Sexual Self. At times, this is the primary self of adolescence, which can overwhelm all other selves. The development of sexual desires is the principal change that separates this period from all that has gone before. Although our sexual behavior is what makes us fully human, it can alienate us from family and friends and take us away from the concerns of school and work. The accompanying fantasies can prevent high school students from concentrating on their studies or even listening in class. Our impulses are not always manageable.

Self-as-Loyal-Friend. The bonds of friendship at adolescence can be stronger than the bonds of family. Many adolescents can confide in friends much more easily than in parents, teachers, or counselors. Their friends are their major refuge from fears and anxieties. If an adolescent has to choose between being with a friend and taking a certain course, attending a certain class, or obeying a parent, the pull from the friend can be much stronger.

Self-in-Peer-Group. The peer group often determines how an adolescent talks, what he eats, what he wears, with whom else he associates, and how hard he works in school. For many, the peer group is the major source of morals and values. These values can come into conflict with those of a friend not in the group, with parents, and with teachers. If one person wants another to cut a class with her, she may resist the temptation. If a group of people do, resistance is lowered. Those who reject the peer group for school or family can become objects of derision.

Self-as-Student. This is what many educators believe should be the primary self of the adolescent in spite of the pull from other selves. The "ideal" high school student takes a full schedule of classes, participates in extracurricular activities in the afternoons, and does three or more hours of homework a night. The typical waking day of the ideal student, therefore, is totally involved in school. In light of the various conflicting selves, it is unrealistic of educators to hold this image up and potentially frustrating for students who won't or can't become part of it.

Self-as-Parent. According to the Children's Defense Fund (1988), 40 percent of the young women who drop out of school cite pregnancy or parenthood as the reason. Many young men see impregnating a girl as a rite of passage. Although the overall rate of births to women aged 15 to 19 has declined in the last 20 years, the rate to unmarried women in that age group has increased. To the 93 percent of the White and the 99 percent of Black women who keep their babies, self-as-parent must become the primary self.

Self-as-My-Work.   Many adolescents, like the ones in this book, do not see any of the "tangible adult tasks," to again cite Erikson (1963), in their lives and do not find many that they are capable of mastering in school. Nor have they cultivated many skills that they can connect with "occupational prototypes" (if, indeed, they have been introduced to any at all).

The adolescent who is bound for college does not need to see "tangible adult tasks" for several years. She has developed some academic skills, but it is not necessary for her to find an occupational prototype to have a sense of self. At this point in her life, she does not need any job skills. The self-as-student will serve her well enough for a few years more. She is in the right place at the right time of her life.

A non-college-bound youth, however, may find himself under greater pressure to develop his self-as-my-work than his more fortunate peers. This pressure puts him in a bind because, with less training, he has fewer work options. Moreover, if he feels inadequate as a learner and does not have a well-developed self-as-student, he may shy away from any kind of job training in the future. The other competing selves except, perhaps, for the self-as-parent cannot add up to a sense of self in general. The entire sense of self for an individual in this predicament is at risk.

RIGHT PLACES AND WRONG PLACES

Educators know quite a bit about the right places for the right students at the right times. The percentage of people going on to higher education has increased through the years. We have ideal schools for ideal students. We teach algebra and trigonometry well to those who become mathematicians; chemistry and physics well to those who become scientists; typing and stenography well to those who become secretaries. But it is educators who have created the right places for the right students. And, by and large, the right students are much like the educators who create the places.

But other students are in the *same* places, and they are in the wrong places. The "wrong" students are going through the same struggles as the "right" students, but their many selves compete differently and become integrated differently. If we are to create the right places for them, we must understand their competing selves. We must also understand why *they* perceive the places we create to be the wrong places.

To answer this question we must find out what the lives of "at-risk" students are like and how school fits into these lives. We must consider what Frederick Erickson (1986) calls the "immediate and local meanings of actions . . . from the actors' point of view" (p. 119). There is a myriad of statistical information available on the dropout phenomenon with which educators have attempted to go from the general to the particular. To get the at-risk student's point of view, however, we have to do the opposite—go from the particular to the general. It is from such a point of view that the young people who make up this book are viewed.

Beginning in the 1986–1987 school year, a cooperative dropout prevention effort, the Stay-in-School Partnership program (sometimes referred to as Mini-College or Mini-School), was launched by the City College of New York, where I teach, and a number of high schools in the city. One of the features of the program was to offer students identified as at risk of dropping out the chance to come to the college once a week and receive high school credit for "high interest" course work.

The schools were public comprehensive high schools attended, for the most part, by low-income Blacks and Hispanics. Students were referred to the program by teachers, administrators, guidance counselors or were self-referrals, and were admitted after an interview with high school staff. All were identified as at risk of dropping out of school and had a history of absences, class cuts, course failures, and/or retention in grade. Their problems with school were similar to the problems that at-risk students have anywhere.

To set up a viable program, we needed to gain some understanding of the population we were dealing with that went beyond attendance records, test scores, promotion records, and guidance referrals. We first needed to know something of their day-to-day lives. Frederick Erickson (1986) advises using an "interpretive" approach based on fieldwork when one is trying to find out what is happening in a particular place. He maintains that the interpretive approach asks different questions than standard approaches to educational research, such as the following:

> What are the conditions of meaning that students and teachers create together, as some students appear to learn and others don't. . . . How is it that it can make sense to students to learn in one situation and not in another? How are these meaning systems created and sustained in daily interaction? (p. 127)

But I wondered if a White, middle-class, middle-aged academic entering a social setting made up of Black and Hispanic adolescents could get valid answers to such questions. Traditionally, anthropologists and others who engage in his type of research have recruited actors from within the setting to act as informants and gather data from them. The use of informants offered a partial solution to the problem of relating to the students but did not deal with the problem of data analysis done from a single subjective point of view. I needed collaborators who could also be involved in the analysis of data, who were intensely interested in the subject population, and who could gather data in situations where I could not. It made sense to draw my collaborators from the population to be studied.

With the help of high school teachers, I recruited three students from the Stay-in-School Partnership program to gather data by collecting tape-recorded "interviews" between themselves and other people of their age on what it was like to be a young person in the city. Each collaborator was to seek out students in their program, other high school students, friends who had dropped out of school. The "interviews" were unstructured and took the form of dialogues rather than information-seeking devices. Each dialogue began with the collaborator's name, date, and a first name for the other person in the dialogue. The collaborator was to explain what he was doing and obtain oral permission to record and publish the data while insuring anonymity.

One of the weaknesses of this first round of the data-gathering process is that I had no female collaborators. Collaborators were to be both male and female, and at various times in the course of the study, there were seven interviewers. Unfortunately, only three worked for the duration of the project and analyzed data, and none of these were women. One student dropped out of school; another was thrown out of her house by a religious parent who decried her desire for worldly goods. A third found it difficult to get cooperation from other students and left the project, and a fourth did only a minimum amount of taping at the end of the data-collection period.

These data and another round of recorded dialogues with different collaborators in the fall of 1987 yielded a total of 91 half-hour dialogues, which were collected from 73 different people. My original three collaborators also recorded high school classes that they considered interesting and others that they considered boring. In addition, they worked with me to analyze data after they had been transcribed. They were able to tell me which of the data they were sure were fabricated by respondents. For this work they were paid $10 an hour.

From the first round of data, my original three collaborators and I put together a collage of voices of youth not oriented toward school. The voices came from people who were quite verbal and able to express their feelings and thoughts. Some of the voices spoke in dialectical variations; most used a street vernacular; some were terse while others were outspoken. To help identify the themes present in the data, I had to rely on my collaborators. Although two of the three had diagnosed reading problems, they seemed to have no difficulty reading the transcriptions on an ongoing basis. I asked each one separately to underline on his copy of the transcriptions what he thought were the most telling comments about school or life in general. Data underlined by all three collaborators were considered the most crucial and analysis focused on these.

The comments consistently singled out by all three collaborators had to do with "pressure" and "boredom." In attempting to be more specific, the four of us tried to separate the material underlined by all three into undefined categories. We decided that the categories spoke to three questions:

1. social pressure (not arising from school),
2. school pressure, and
3. boredom (in school).

The first category included family pressure, sexual pressure, pressures from peers or the life of the streets, pressures about jobs and future work. School did not alleviate these pressures; in fact, it only seemed to create more. Moreover, most of what goes on in classes was judged as boring. This judgment was reinforced from student to student. Boredom appeared to be a reaction to school pressure that enabled a student internally to drop out. These conclusions were summarized in an article with my three collaborators as co-authors, "Giving Voice to High School Students: Pressure and Boredom, Ya Know What I'm Sayin'?" (Farrell, Peguero, Lindsey, and White, 1988).

After the second round of data collection, it became clear that the pressures my collaborators identified emanated from the pressure of competing selves. Our dialogues suggest that this population's inability to integrate these selves into one identity is the overarching problem that accounts for the dropout phenomena, and this inability is the major theme of this book. The following chapters, then, will look at the competing selves of at-risk students in (as much as possible) the students' own words. I will point out the social mechanisms that affect self-development, and suggest ways schools can help adolescents attain this integration of selves.

THE PLAN OF THE BOOK

Chapter 1, "The Career Self," will explore the future occupational projections of young people within a changing economic climate. Their perceptions of the world of work will be investigated as will what they believe their prospects to be. We will look at their anxieties about the future and how their projections differ from the realities of the world of work as gleaned from recent sociological data.

Chapter 2, "The Sexual Self," will discuss the pressures that both young men and women feel from their peers as well as from their own impulses to engage in sexual behavior. The subjects discuss how those pressures affect them on school-related matters. They will speak to their fears of AIDS and pregnancy. We will also look at the kinds of knowledge they have about sexuality and their attitudes toward alternative sexual orientations.

Chapter 3, "Self Among Peers," will investigate both the self-as-loyal-friend and the self-in-peer-group. Loyalty to friends is the dominant value alluded to by the students interviewed; indeed, friendship is the strongest bonding force in their lives. The importance of friends to these young people will be compared to the importance of parents, teachers, and counselors. Lawrence Kohlberg's (1981) theories of moral development will be applied to the value systems of our respondents. How peer subcultures affect student attitudes and achievement will also be discussed.

Both the supportive and the inhibiting factors of the family will be the subjects of Chapter 4, "The Family Self." We consider how the at-risk adolescents in our sample perceive their families; they may see them as adversarial but not as nonexistent. And the values of their families are most often the values of the larger society. We will also look at how single-parent and extended families cope with problems of living.

Chapter 5, "Self-as-Parent," discusses possible reasons why young women become pregnant and how schools could better cope with this phenomenon. Lack of knowledge about contraception does not seem to be the major cause of pregnancy; women in different subcultures or social classes must often order their life events differently. This chapter will document how becoming a mother was a positive force in the life of one young unmarried woman in high school.

What society believes should be the primary identity of young people is the subject of Chapter 6, "The Student Self." The inadequacies of this self will be contrasted with the attractions of the competing selves. The main thrust of this chapter will be student perceptions of school. The distribution of grades in school is compared to the distribution of income in the larger economic system. We will also discuss how student experience in elementary school affects that of secondary school.

Chapter 7, "Boredom," speaks to the results of the inadequacy of the self-as-student. The premise is that boredom is a mental state that is socially constructed, as defined by Peter Berger and Thomas Luckmann (1967). Boredom seems to be both a way of internally dropping out of school and one of a series of steps to physically dropping out. There are also indications that it is a result of the process as well as the content of teaching. Boredom is linked to the pressure students feel because they are so often judged inadequate.

Chapter 8, "Drugs," deals with the ever-present spectre of substance abuse. Most of the respondents used some illegal substance at one time or another even though they were aware of the pitfalls. The chapter investigates why young people use drugs. While conducting this research, we became sharply aware that the prevalence and low price of the drug "crack" has made the narcotics problem greater than ever. We also address the conviction that some students have that drugs are one path to financial success.

Chapter 9, "Conflicting Meanings of School," contrasts the culture of the teacher who owes his livelihood to his education to the culture of the prospective dropout. Dialogues between students and teachers demonstrate clashes of values. We see how students who accept the values of teachers are ostracized and looked down on by those who do not. The "meaning systems" of teachers will be contrasted to the "meaning systems" of students.

The final chapter, "Learning in a Real-World Context," offers solutions to the problem. The solutions offered link education with work and describe models that have been successfully implemented. That these solutions involve structural changes in our system of schooling and delegate more responsibility to teachers might make them unworkable to some. I describe three actual projects, two of which were successfully developed in tandem with a regular school program, the other an alternative school that, I believe, failed.

The order of the first six chapters follows the self-development theory I proposed in what seemed to be the order of importance to our respondents. Erikson (1963), of course, thinks the formation of an occupational identity, or what I call the "career self," is the major task of the adolescent. Many adolescents, however, are most concerned with their sexual selves and that became the subject of the second chapter. Peers seemed to have more immediate impact on these young peoples' lives than their families. We will see that the self-as-parent might become the major force in some young women's lives but that others are completely unaffected by it. To the at-risk, the student self pales by comparison with the preceding selves.

Boredom makes up a separate chapter because it is the most frequently heard complaint about school. The impact of drugs did not manifest itself in our dialogues from the beginning but emerged as the most destructive force in these peoples' lives after analyzing all the data. This became the subject of an unplanned Chapter 8. The conflicting meanings of school to teachers and to students are the major problem that educators will have to deal with in devising solutions to the dropout problem. Appropriately, solutions are saved until the last chapter.

1

The Career Self

MICHAEL: There's always an opportunity of getting jobs.
COLLABORATOR: Oh, yeah, there is!
MICHAEL: Fast-food restaurant.
COLLABORATOR: But let's say you're a grownup and 21 years old.
   You don't live with your parents any more and everything, and
   I don't think you're gonna live by $3.35 an hour. You know, I
   don't think somebody that old or somebody that has to buy
   clothing, food, and he has a girlfriend and he wants to get married or he wants to support his wife, I don't think $3.35 an hour
   or four something an hour is gonna support himself.
MICHAEL: But somebody that's 21 years old and doesn't have a
   job, they put themselves in that situation; cuz if they dropped
   out of high school when they were 17, they had to go from then
   till 21 to get a job, ya know what I'm sayin'? Just, you know,
   just go down there and get something going.
COLLABORATOR: But it's not everybody who's like that. It's not
   that easy.
MICHAEL: All you gotta do is apply yourself. Cuz like what I'm
   doin' is taking the Civil Service. I filled out an application for
   the Post Office. And hopefully, I can find out when the Transit
   Authority test is coming up. I'll take that.
COLLABORATOR: But don't you have to be a high school graduate?
MICHAEL: But they don't call you up like for three years. So I
   would be out of here by three years.
COLLABORATOR: I'm not sayin' that can't happen. That's smart for
   you to do. Like when you get out of high school and stuff, you
   have to force yourself and everything. But I'm sayin' it's not the
   same for everyone. The same thing won't happen to everyone.
   Not everybody's like that. Not everybody's like that. You know
   you drop out of school; sometimes people don't think about it.
   Sometimes people just think of . . .

MICHAEL: But if somebody drops out of school they must think of,
    you know they gotta think about it. Say, whattam I gonna do
    when I get outa here. You know, if I drop out what I'm gonna
    do. Cuz they, I know they don't just drop out and say, "Well, I
    can get a job anywhere." I don't think it's like that.
COLLABORATOR: I don't think it's like that either.
MICHAEL: Cuz you know the thing that scares me the most is
    fuckin' havin' no future. That really scares me. . . . One of my
    greatest fears is growin' up and bein' a bum. . . . Cuz you know
    them niggers look sorry as shit. . . . Sometimes I be lookin' at
    them . . . and I be like damn, that might be me in twenty-five
    years, man. . . . How the fuck can you be happy with no
    money? You have to beg niggers for fifty cents. Damn, what
    the fuck is this?

THE DREAM AND THE NIGHTMARE

I do not know what the antecedent of Michael's "this" is in the last
sentence. Even though he brings in the image of the street beggar, he
does not seem to sense that there might be something wrong with the
larger socioeconomic system in that there are beggars at all. While
many of the respondents in the dialogues were critical of school and
teachers, none spoke to inequalities in the larger society. It seemed
that, like Michael, they had to believe that they had the chance to
succeed, even though they sensed at some level that society could
easily turn their dream of success into a nightmare.

The adolescent, to cite again Erik Erikson (1963), tries to integrate
what has gone before in her life with her new social roles. Successful
integration, at this stage, is marked by the promise of a career. Her
identity crystallizes around a future occupation. But in order for this to
happen, the individual must have established a relationship with the
world of skills and tools. In many cases, however, this has not happened.

School success, which few in this at-risk population has experienced, is a function of the development of literacy in its widest sense.
Literacy, certainly, is one of the primary skills needed to gain access to
the technology of our society. But it is not just a matter of being
literate; it has to do with how *much* print literacy, how *much* mathe-
matical literacy, how *much* computer literacy, etc., one has. By and
large, the at-risk school population has less of these commodities than
other students.

School success, nonetheless, is also largely determined by attitudes. There have been special education students who have earned

high school diplomas, more through sustained endeavor and teacher support than by the development of literacy. In the preadolescent school years, Erikson says, the child must develop a sense of "industry." One way of developing this is by experiencing work completion. Students must see their completed products and feel good about them. Unless that happens, school is toil but not meaningful work.

The adolescent, then, for whom school has been toil and who has achieved a limited amount of literacy and industry may have a difficult time deciding on a future career. Many in our sample avoided the question of a career when asked. One young man, asked what he planned on doing in the future, responded, "live." Another said, "Well . . . I don't really think about it. I just think, now. You know, now. That's my time. Maybe in the future I'll think of the future, ya know what I'm sayin'?"

One dialogue brought an angry response. One of my collaborators on two occasions interviewed two students whom he called "nerds." The nerds were freshmen who did not dress "cool," who achieved in school, and who expressed positive attitudes toward teachers and courses. They were considered fair game by my collaborators who delighted in "snapping" (verbally dueling) with them. On one occasion, after being subjected to several minutes of insults about their clothing and their attitudes toward school, one of the nerds retaliated with, "I bet you don't even know what college you're going to. I bet you haven't even considered what you're going to do after high school."

My collaborator, who usually got the better of such encounters, became angry and responded with, "I'm gonna go where life takes me, okay?"

The angry response indicates a deliberate avoidance of the subject of future prospects rather than indifference to it. The question then arises of how aware these students are of the world of work. Do their "meaning systems" or realities correspond to the realities of the marketplace? Would the credentials they can show for entrance to the world of gainful employment impress prospective employers? One young man claimed to be making a living as a semiprofessional boxer while attending high school, but he was aware that he did not have sufficient ability to ensure a promising career in the ring. He volunteered that he would like to be an architect, a profession he seemed to know little about and for which he was not able to judge his abilities.

Another wanted to find work as a model, while pursuing a singing and acting career. At the time he was interviewed, he was working part-time as a busboy in a restaurant. Although he was strikingly handsome, he did not realize that he needed to obtain a photographer's portfolio simply to start looking for work as a model. Neither did he know about acting schools, although New York has many and prerequisites are not always required for admission. He was 17 years old and had been retained in grade twice. His chances to earn a diploma were not great.

One of my collaborators has a dream of being a disc jockey. He and his older brother have enough sound equipment and records to "DJ" at parties. One afternoon, when I was to meet him and my other two collaborators at his home to analyze data, I arrived to find my collaborator eagerly refining his dream. His brother, a friend, and he had been up all night talking. Apparently, a motorcycle club had seen and heard them DJ-ing at a party and had approached them about the possibility of DJ-ing and managing a private club that the motorcycle group wanted to open. Although the club was only a possibility, the three had spent hours enthusiastically discussing such details as how to screen people at the door of "their" club, what kind of equipment to get, and who would do what job. The club has not yet opened.

In a class I was teaching of at-risk students in our Stay-in-School Partnership program, I asked my students what they wanted to do for work. The majority did not have answers, so I then asked them what kinds of work did they think were available. A number mentioned construction. At the time there was a large construction project at City College that the high school students had to go by each time they came to class. Several students were convinced that they could be construction workers if they wanted to. None of these students had very much experience with hand tools but, even more importantly, they did not have access to people who currently held these jobs and were not aware of the necessity of belonging to a union. Later, a dialogue with one of my collaborators showed that he had similar beliefs.

COLLABORATOR: Like this guy I know, he's a construction worker. He says that I could get a job if I took a GED, as a laborer working, make like $300 a week. So I figure if somebody graduates, they could do the same thing.

EF: But can anybody get those jobs?

COLLABORATOR: Yeah, they could. As a laborer, construction. (*Pause*) All you need to do is go to like a two-week course on how to do your job, and when you go to work on . . .

EF: What two-week class?

COLLABORATOR: You know, like a two-week class on, um, in like welding, or a two-week course in construction, carpentry, something like that.

EF: But who teaches that? I don't know of one.

COLLABORATOR: Schools. I don't know. I forgot the name. Schools. I got a list at home.

EF: Okay, don't you have to be on the union?

COLLABORATOR: I'm not sure you have to be anything.

In fact, it is extremely difficult to get construction jobs in New York City. They pay well and their number is limited. You must know someone in a position of influence or, better yet, have a relative to help you get such a job. There are a number of proprietary schools in the city that offer courses, which are considerably longer in duration than two weeks, in the skilled trades but they are expensive and cannot ensure employment. The majority of people who begin in these schools never complete the course.

The students in our dialogues did not get a great deal of career counseling in school. In their dreams, they did not seem to be aware of the realities of the job market. But Michael's nightmare about being a street beggar and the refusal of many respondents to think about the future demonstrate that they might, on some level, know all too well that they have limited knowledge and skills to sell.

THE REALITIES OF THE JOB MARKET

With little knowledge of how their abilities fit into the job market or even what their abilities are, our respondents are at a distinct disadvantage in making career decisions. They believe that there are jobs for them, as evidenced by Michael's dream, but they have only inklings of their inferior status in the market. These inklings keep surfacing in the dialogues.

COLLABORATOR: What choo wanta do in the summer?

BOBBY: Well, in the summertime, I will hopefully . . . I will hopefully this summer, I'll get a job. You know, like, I'm really slackin' the shit off now, gettin' old as a bitch, man. You know what I'm sayin', man? Bein' seventeen in New York is a motherfucker. If you ain't got no job, you're fucked. And that shit is pitiful, man. You know what I'm sayin' man? Shit. God Damn, shit, shit.

COLLABORATOR: Wait a minute, why're you cursin' so much?

BOBBY: I don't know, man, shit.

What is the nature of the job market that seems to confound these students? William Julius Wilson (1987) has assembled some alarming statistics in his analysis of economic conditions in the inner city and how those conditions affect urban families and individuals. Wilson considers the major factor in recent social change to be the dramatic loss of low and semiskilled jobs, as service-producing replace goods-producing industries. This change affects the country as a whole but especially the cities. From 1970 to 1984, New York City lost 492,000 jobs that required less than a high school education and gained 239,000 jobs in which the average employee had some higher education.

In the same period during which these economic changes have been happening, inner-city neighborhoods have experienced more crime, joblessness, out-of-wedlock births, female-headed families, and welfare dependency. As late as the 1960s, Wilson asserts, these neighborhoods were vertically integrated with lower, working, and, in the Black community, middle-class families. Since the 1970s, however, the middle-class families have abandoned the cities for the suburbs and working-class families have disappeared along with their jobs. This abandonment and disappearance has had profound effects on those who remain in the inner cities.

One of the most profound affects, according to Wilson, is that the people left in the inner cities have become "socially isolated from mainstream patterns of behavior" (p. 60). By social isolation he means the lack of contact with people who represent mainstream society. In the inner city, Wilson suggests that

> social isolation also generates behavior not conducive to good work histories. The patterns of behavior that are associated with a life of casual work (tardiness and absenteeism) are quite different from those that accompany a life of regular or steady work (e.g., the habit of waking up early in the morning to a ringing alarm clock). In neighborhoods in which nearly every family has at least one person who is steadily employed, the norms and behavior patterns that emanate from a life of regularized employment become part of the community gestalt. (pp. 60–61)

Tardiness and absenteeism are symptomatic of the at-risk high school population. When asked what one thing he would change about his dropout prevention program, one student responded:

> For them not to be callin' my house should I be absent, wantin' to know if I'm gonna come in the next day. If I'm there, I'm

there. If I'm not, I'm not. I don't like to be waked up 7:00 in
the morning askin' me if I'm gonna come. I know where the
school is, you know. I don't need help gettin' there.

It cannot be said that this student's attitudes necessarily reflect a
"community gestalt." It may be that school itself does not offer him
any valid reasons to improve his attendance or that he resents authority. School may have little meaning to him. But Wilson (1987) believes
it is socioeconomic factors that largely determine whether school is
meaningful. The middle- and working-class families that no longer
exist in the inner city provided "mainstream role models that . . . keep
alive the perception that education is meaningful" (p. 61). The high
school student may still see dropouts, according to Wilson, but if he
also sees working people he might "see a connection between education and meaningful employment" (p. 60).

John Ogbu (1978) attributes economic conditions to racial rather
than class stratification. Certain minority groups, particularly Blacks,
have a caste-like status that is extremely difficult to overcome. The
caste-like minorities, Ogbu believes, are denied social mobility by what
he calls the "job ceiling." Because of their caste status these minorities are
not permitted to compete freely for jobs for which they are qualified
and are excluded from the most desirable jobs. Jobs are therefore
divided into two categories: those above the ceiling and those below it.

The following dialogue represents typical thinking about work
among our respondents.

COLLABORATOR: Do you, are you working now?
ROY: Well, just recently I got fired from my job.
COLLABORATOR: Oh, what job was that?
ROY: I don't wanna specify.
COLLABORATOR (*laughing*):   Okay, what was the reason for you
    being fired?
ROY: Cuz I disliked the manager.
COLLABORATOR: Oh, you disliked the manager. What did he do to
    make you dislike him?
ROY: He's a pain in the ass!
COLLABORATOR: Oh, so he kicked you in the butt, huh?
ROY: No, not exactly. See but, he's the type person wants to make
    you work like you're makin' five dollars an hour, when you're
    only makin' minimum wage.

That Roy did not want to say what his job was indicates an
awareness of his status. Another student, Lee, when asked what her job

was replied with a question, "Do I have to say it? McDonald's." From the dialogue at the beginning of the chapter, it can be seen that these students are quite aware of the inadequacy of the minimum wage and, moreover, seemed embarrassed to admit that they have such jobs. Jobs like these become hard to endure and easy to quit.

Whether the job situation is a function of a declining manufacturing base or whether it is caused by racism is a debatable point. Wilson (1987) presents persuasive evidence to support his thesis, but both he and Ogbu (1978) would agree that young people without education and skills lack access to the job network. That was certainly the case among the students in our dialogues and those in my class. Other than low-paying service jobs, they do not know what jobs are available or how to get or train for them. This applies both to part-time jobs now or careers later.

One wonders, of course, whether there is a job network at all for the at-risk student to access. Other than the vague "guy I know" who told my collaborator the dubious story that he could get a construction job after a two-week course, the only other reference to the job network that appears in all our data is Michael's mention of civil service tests. In New York City, there is a weekly newspaper devoted entirely to civil service jobs. None of the students in the high school class I taught had ever heard of it before I mentioned it.

My college students, on the other hand, most of whom live in the inner city, are generally aware of what civil service jobs they are qualified for and when examinations are given. Very often, someone in their family has one of these jobs. This is probably one of the few job networks in the inner city. But even if the at-risk high school students had access to this network, many civil service jobs require a high school diploma and some degree of literacy. They simply may not be able to pass the tests.

The reality of the job market, then, for the at-risk students is (1) there are few jobs available for them, (2) those that are available are minimum-wage service jobs, (3) they have few skills and little knowledge to sell on the market, and (4) they have little access to whatever job network there is.

CAREERS

The word "career" was never used in our dialogues. The word "job" was frequently used. Our respondents apparently do not see any job they are likely to get as their lifework. They do not have clear visions of the future and they look to their peers rather than to their teachers and counselors for guidance.

Differing Visions of the Future

When asked what they would like to do after high school, our students gave such responses as actor, singer, model, basketball player, fashion designer, disc jockey. No one said doctor, lawyer, or engineer, although the boxer wanted to be an architect. Obviously, they identify with whom or what is visible to them. However, they choose their favored careers precisely because they are not close to them. The semiprofessional boxer did not say he wanted to be the light heavyweight champion of the world; he knew enough about the sport to assess his abilities.

It may be understandable why no one named a profession as a future career, but no one named plumber, carpenter, or mechanic, either. Even though construction jobs in the city are hard to get, employment possibilities for skilled tradesmen, nationwide, are good and wages relatively high. But if Wilson (1987) is correct, these students may encounter few tradesmen in their daily lives. What then of vocational schooling? Some areas of the country, and certainly New York City, have some excellent vocational schools. Attending such schools was not a consideration, however, for the students in our dialogues.

Vocational education on the high school level requires a relatively early career choice for the people in our dialogues, sometimes in the eighth or ninth grade. With no role models, few students have motivations for such early decisions. Moreover, the better schools require certain academic abilities or special talents. Some vocational schools are extremely difficult to get into; recently, the Board of Education in New York dictated that some vacancies would be filled by lottery. The at-risk students in our dialogues had neither the incentive nor knowledge to make vocational decisions at a young age, and they report little vocational counseling in their junior high school years.

Not one respondent identified with a definite occupation. In a comprehensive high school there is often no incentive to do so. Certainly, the college-bound student does not have to; she can identify with her future education. I have found college-bound students in the inner city, however, who identify with both a college and a career. As well as teaching a class of at-risk students, I alternately teach a class of very able students who attend an excellent comprehensive high school on the City College campus. The contrast between the groups is stark.

The A. Philip Randolph Campus High School is a comprehensive public high school located at City College. The socioeconomic and ethnic makeup is very similar to that of the schools that are part of the Stay-in-School Partnership. Although Campus High School does not have an entrance examination, its students must either be recommended by a guidance counselor in their previous school or demonstrate some kind of academic ability. The school has a low dropout rate, and virtually all its graduates attend college.

The school's curriculum is rigorous and the teachers demanding. The foundation that funded the school in its initial stages was interested in increasing minority student enrollment in medical schools. Although medicine is no longer the dominant interest of the students, everyone in my classes saw his future in one of the professions. Each of the students in my classes had developed Erikson's "sense of industry." They had tools and skills.

Most of the students I have taught in Campus High School had very specific ideas about what they wanted to do. My course was an introduction to education for those who might want to be teachers. Few, however, were interested in teaching as anything but a backup career. Typical responses to the question of what they want to do include medicine and maybe teaching if the student did not get into medical school; law with business as a backup; and psychology. One student wanted a specific high-level administrative job with the Board of Education in New York that he thought he could get if he first became an attorney; his mother was a teacher.

These students knew what their abilities were, knew something about the job market, and saw the relationship of school to their career. They knew it was through education that they would gain access to the job network. Self-as-student and self-as-my-work were well-developed selves for them with little distinction between these selves. Like their at-risk peers, they did not envision themselves as skilled tradesmen. Unlike them, they were not haunted by the nightmare of their becoming street beggars.

Whereas all seniors at Campus High School have to take a college-level course and while most take it at City College, few wish to pursue degrees there. They prefer out-of-town colleges or colleges considered more prestigious to the general public. They do have a common desire with my City College teacher-education students, however; none of the people in either group see themselves as living in the city after graduation from college, even though most of the City College students will work there. These groups will be part of the minority middle class that Wilson (1987) speaks of as abandoning the inner city.

What makes the at-risk students differ from those at City College or at Campus High School? Is it simply a question of academic ability? Is it supportive families? Is it the right kind of encouragement from teachers? Obviously, it is all of these things. The students from Campus High School have had more academic success than their at-risk peers. They read assignments and write papers when asked. But we do not know a great deal about their relative abilities when they entered kindergarten. As I suggested in the last chapter, it does not seem reasonable to assume that the large number of students who drop out of school simply lack the ability to graduate.

It is not reasonable to assume that only the Campus High School students have supportive families; nonetheless, the Campus students undoubtedly get a great deal more encouragement from their high school. We do not know a great deal about their lives before high school, but Campus students report having had to ignore certain peer pressures in the past. Attitudes toward work and careers are formed by peers as well as by teachers and parents.

Peers and Careers

It is precisely at the time that students are to make vocational school choices and decide on high schools that peer pressure is first reported to exert itself powerfully. One of my collaborators asked a young man named Maleek what some of his hobbies were.

MALEEK: Sewing, drawing.
COLLABORATOR: You like to *sew*?
MALEEK: Yeah, I like to sew. Sewing is great, man. Sewing is great for a hobby, man. I also like . . .
COLLABORATOR: Man, you know your hobbies, stop bullshitting.
MALEEK: All right. Women. That's a good hobby. Yeah, I like womans as a hobby . . .

The speakers continued to talk and joke about women and sex. Maleek and my collaborator had a good time and established a rapport. But Maleek was pressured to avoid the topic of sewing. I assume it was not considered macho enough. However, the respondents in the dialogues were very fashion-conscious and they knew that many fashion designers are men. But, of course, they didn't personally know any men who were in the fashion industry. Even though this is a shrinking industry in New York, it is one of the few manufacturing segments left. At any rate, with the help of my collaborator and the mediated assurance of anonymity, I sought out Maleek to interview him.

EF: Let me ask you, can you tell me about your future in the next three or four years? We won't hold you to this.
MALEEK: I hopefully could get a job. You know, be an independent businessman. That's what I hope to have, my own business. It's something no one can take away from you, ya know what I'm sayin'? And I'd like to make clothes and be like a fashion designer, that's like if I get that far.
EF: Are you doing anything like that now?
MALEEK: I was gonna be in a fashion show, but I had to drop out. I had to buy a lawyer.

Maleek was reluctant to tell me about his legal problems and I did not push him. From what I could gather he became spontaneously involved in some infraction of the law when he was out with friends. The end result was that the case was dismissed. By then the fashion show, which was school-sponsored but in which participants would model their own clothes, had passed. Maleek has not pursued his dream since then.

In the New York public school system there is an excellent vocational school, the High School of Fashion Design. Until the quota of randomly selected admissions mentioned above was implemented, admission was based on previous school history and talent. Maleek claims to have never heard of this school when he was in junior high, and even if he had he would not have been ready to submit any examples of what he could do with his application. Also, his previous academic record weighed against him.

I cannot say whether he has any talent in the area of fashion design, but he had no role models and knew no one who worked in the industry. Students from the inner city who have any such knowledge are likely to have mothers or sisters who work on sewing machines; young males most likely push cartloads of garments through the streets for the minimum wage. Education would give Maleek his only access to that network, but he missed his chance to go to the most appropriate school for his choice of work.

With his enthusiasm for sewing Maleek could have developed his career self, but he lacked the appropriate support, and his main identity is now primarily a peer self. The students at Campus High School have largely rejected the peer groups of their neighborhoods; many have found new, college-bound peer groups in their high school. If their academic work does not hold up, however, they go back to the high school that serves their neighborhood and lose their newfound groups. They then have to rely on their old peer groups to support their student and career selves.

The peer groups for the at-risk students also support the sexual self. My collaborator in the dialogue above readily accepted Maleek's sexual self but had a difficult time with Maleek as fashion designer, a possible career self. Dialogues about students' current work often disparaged the jobs. For the Campus High School students, peer groups do not increase the conflict over competing selves; for the at-risk students, they often do.

Teachers and Careers

By and large, high school teachers are not trained to be career counselors. English teachers are trained in language, literature, and how to teach; social studies teachers are trained in their appropriate content areas and how to teach them, etc. Even vocational education teachers do little counseling outside their fields and few of the at-risk students in our data pool had ever had any such counseling. Guidance counselors are few and far between and are more interested in school adjustment problems than in career counseling.

Valerie Lee and Ruth Ekstrom (1987), using a data base of 12,000 students found that guidance services were not equally distributed among all students. Students from lower socioeconomic status or minority status in their sample had less access to guidance counseling. In *The Shopping Mall High School*, Arthur Powell, Eleanor Farrar, and David Cohen (1985) see counseling as a consumer good. They quote a parent describing the situation as "The reach is from the student to the school and not the other way. . . . The arrows don't go both ways" (p. 48). The students in the Stay-in-School Partnership, as will be seen in a later chapter, do not seek out guidance counselors.

Teachers in dropout-prevention programs have volunteered for their assignments but, for the most part, have had no special training and must rely on their own resourcefulness. The emphasis of such programs is obviously to keep people in school rather than to prepare them for work. They are likely to want to teach basic skills and to try to build interest for school subjects or subjects that can be translated into school credits. The self that teachers offer is a student self rather than a career self.

One teacher in the Stay-in-School Partnership lists his priorities as
(1) keeping students in school, and (2) helping them gain as many
basic skills as possible before they drop out. One cannot argue that
teaching basic skills is not essential, but one wonders whether such an
endeavor is worthwhile from the student's perspective if the only jobs
available to dropouts are minimum-wage service jobs.

Teachers teach what has worked for them, not what is likely to
work for at-risk students. An English teacher, for example, makes her
living with literature; the vast majority of her students cannot. But for
many English teachers, to do other than teach English in a classroom
would be very difficult. The teacher might substitute career education
pamphlets and the like for reading material, but few are willing to
build a curriculum around this and take the necessary second step,
showing the student actual workplaces and introducing them to employees and employers. Most teachers' primary responsibilities call on
them to remain in the classroom for the largest part of the day.

That English teacher may rightly feel that she must see that her
students have the highest degree of print literacy possible, so that they
may function in the world of work. At the end of the course I taught to
at-risk students, I suggested to them that perhaps my class on "What It
Is Like To Be A Young Person In The City" did not help them very
much. Perhaps, I suggested, I should have made them write every day
in class and require them to do compositions at home so, by the end of
the course, they would be able to write good English. Every one of
them said they would not have registered for the course had that been
the case.

While their attitude might seem to stem from laziness, it is not
illogical. If I were told that I would have to learn to sight-read music (I
am partially tone-deaf) or learn Russian (I was never a good foreign
language student) as prerequisite to a situation, I would avoid the
situation. Although these skills are important, I see no payoff in them
at this time in my life. Neither would they improve my professional
life. Moreover, I do not think reading music would increase my appre-
ciation of Mozart, and I can read Dostoyevski in translation. I cannot
guarantee to these students that being able to write compositions
would get them jobs.

WORK

None of the students in the dialogues had found any kind of present or
future work to identify with. Only the boxer had been able to try on a

work identity for size. What has happened to these students is that the
student self and the career self—the two most promising selves and the
selves that society values for adolescents—are the selves least developed in them. The career self especially could be the self that would
lead these young people out of the wrong place or might transform
some part of that place into the right place.

Erikson (1963) reports that when Sigmund Freud was asked what
the ingredients for a happy life were, he replied, "to love and to work"
(p. 265). School is not preparing them to do either, but that can
possibly be remedied. What is most frustrating, however, is that there
might not be any work for these young people to do, and they are only
beginning to find this out.

One of my collaborators engaged another young man, Maurice, in
a dialogue on jobs. Maurice seemed like a perceptive young man, but
he had been retained in grade twice. He was in one of the dropout
prevention programs that made up the Stay-in-School Partnership.
Maurice commented:

> I think it's very hard for people who have come out of school
> and drop out, and they really don't have that much experience
> in a job, you know, in getting working. Cuz there's a lot of jobs
> that you need experience in. Like you go out and look for a
> job, and I've gone out before and looked for a job, and I know
> how to do the job, but I haven't had another job with expe-
> rience, or I haven't come out of school, or they need someone
> who works full-time and stuff like that. There's always some
> problem. So either you need experience or something and I
> think a person who drops out and doesn't have a GED or any-
> thing, I think it's very hard for them to get a job.

I would have liked to have interviewed Maurice myself but I was
unable to. Shortly after this dialogue took place, he dropped out of
school. No one seemed to know where he was or what he was doing.

2

The Sexual Self

"My dad, when he was 17 I was born. I was born when he was 17, so you know, I haven't even got a girl pregnant. I'm 17 and I haven't even had a girlfriend yet," reported a young man to support his premise that the teenage years were the hardest in one's life.

Two of my collaborators later engaged in conversation two young women they knew who were also in the Stay-in-School Partnership. The talk went from relationships to fidelity to sex. One of the women complained of boys' bragging about their sexual conquests.

LORNA: I'm not askin' one person; I'm askin' all of you, all! Why is it a must? Y'all have to, you're all in a group, right? Y'all don't have to be. . . . Y'all don't have sex one time in your life but ya all have to sit there and say, "Yeah, I did this with this girl. I had sex." Why y'all think sex make you all men?

MARCIA: Let the men answer that question.

COLLABORATOR 1: You're saying', suppose I'm talkin to you and I go tell somebody else, "Yeah, me and her had sex, I had sex, blah, blah, blah?"

LORNA: Yeah, and you never had sex.

COLLABORATOR 2: Why? Why do guys do that? Because one, they haven't been with too many girls and, "Boy, I'm lucky, let the whole block know." Then they don't want to look dumb in front of their friends. (*Pause*) Okay, that's just like you're in a group and you can't read and somebody says, "Read this book," and you feel like a total idiot. Everybody else, they might have, and he's over there, "Well, like, uh, I didn't. . . ." He feels stupid. Of course he gonna say, I got her.

MARCIA: So there's a lot of pressure for guys to have sex?

COLLABORATOR 1: Yeah, you girls got nothing to worry about. You all ain't gotta talk about nothing to nobody.

LORNA: Let me tell you where we get the pressure from with girls.
We get the pressure from y'all. We all get the pressure cuz y'all
give us the name. Now let's say you tell me your friends, and
we her. . . . And they want their chance, and they pass it
around.

BOYS AND GIRLS TOGETHER

What is the place of sex in the lives of these young people? Apparently,
if a young man has sex he gains status with his peers. The first young
man in the examples above seemed to see it as a rite of passage. It is
interesting that my collaborator's offhand comment equated sex with
literacy. Not having sex is like not knowing how to read; one has to
hide the fact. In Chapter 1, I referred to literacy as a commodity that
this population has less of than others. It might be that the young men
of this population are less sexually active than news media treatment
of adolescent pregnancy and venereal disease would have us believe.
In the case of young women, because I had no female collaborators,
this is less clear.

What is clear is that sex is what changes adolescence from all that
has gone before. For the people in our sample, and for all the people
of their age, it is still a very new thing. They have only been dealing
with it for three to four years. It is the *sine qua non* of their fantasies; it
can give both status and disgrace; it constantly confronts them in
media and in advertisements. With it comes the fear of pregnancy and
AIDS. Yet there is nothing in school that can compete with its mys-
tique.

Two years before my collaborators and I collected data, Michele
Fine (1985, 1986, 1987, 1988) conducted an ethnography at one of the
schools that became part of the Stay-in-School Partnership. Her extremely interesting and perceptive article on "Sexuality, Schooling,
and Adolescent Females" (1988) was subtitled, "The Missing Discourse of Desire." Fine found very little discussion of sexuality by
young women.

In classroom discussions, girls who were heterosexually active rarely
spoke, for fear of being ostracized. Those who were heterosexual
virgins had the same worry. And most students who were gay,
bisexual, or lesbian remained closeted, aware of the very real
dangers of homophobia. (1988, p. 49)

What I suspect from the data gathered by my collaborators is that the experiences of the sexual selves of young men in this population differ from those of young women. Gender attitudes toward sexuality and relationships differ. Moreover, actual sexual behaviors differ between genders. Few boys seek girlfriends; girls would like to have boyfriends.

The Boys

In only three places in all the dialogues collected did boys actually use the word "girlfriend." One was in the dialogue at the beginning of this chapter. It is not clear just what the young man meant by the term. Did he want someone to have a long-term relationship with as his father did with his mother? Or did he just want someone to sleep with? To impregnate? We cannot be sure, but it seems that a "girlfriend" was not the primary part of his yearning.

Another use of the term "girlfriend" was in "The Dream and the Nightmare" dialogue in Chapter 1. My collaborator suggests to Michael that the minimum wage is inadequate if someone "has a girlfriend and he wants to get married or he wants to support his wife. . . ." In this case the girlfriend is in the future. There is also a realization that the financial situation these young men find themselves in or project for themselves may not permit a permanent relationship.

The third use of the term was in a dialogue in which another of my collaborators was questioning a young man, Syl, on his use of drugs. He asked him what he would do if his parents found out about his drug use.

SYL: If they do, I'll just run away.
COLLABORATOR: Where would you run away?
SYL: I'll just go to a girlfriend's house.
COLLABORATOR: Oh, so you have girlfriends, girl *friends*, right?
SYL: Yeah, girlfriends. You gotta have more than one.
COLLABORATOR: Just in case one drops you, right?
SYL: No, cuz they're all full of shit.

This kind of contempt for women was evidenced elsewhere in the dialogues. There were two other young men who claimed to be sexually active, but my collaborators did not believe them. They did believe Syl (one knew him) and another young man who claimed to have four different women in the last week. It is interesting to note that the two who were believed were heavy drug users. The young man who had the four women said they were a problem because they might get pregnant.

COLLABORATOR: You think girls are a problem, right?
MARC: Yeah, because right now I don't care about girls now. Just like having sex with 'em and throw 'em out and like to keep on having a good time, you know.

None of the young men in the dialogues mentioned having a current girlfriend in a mutually exclusive relationship and only one seemed to want to have one. Is it that they are not ready for relationships or is it that young women are not available to them? It might be that at-risk high school males without jobs are not the most attractive partners for high school women. In one dialogue one of my collaborators was talking with a friend about a girl with whom the friend had formerly had a short-term involvement. When my collaborator asked him what grade she was in, his friend replied, "Another eighth-grade bitch."

Does the fact that she was "another" imply that eighth graders make up a large part of the pool of women available to these young men? Assuming that men tend to become involved with younger women, it may well be that there is a scarcity of women even if the men of this age desired to have relationships. Women may be interested in older men or men with more status. My collaborator's equating sex with literacy may not be far from the truth; this male population may have less of both these commodities than other students.

Who are the women that reportedly do have sex with our male respondents? In the aforementioned conversation among my two collaborators and two female participants in their program, when one of the women complained about boys bragging to their friends about whom they had sex with, one of my collaborators offered an explanation.

COLLABORATOR 1:   There's a lot of freakin' girls out there, though.
LORNA: What's freaky?
COLLABORATOR 1:   Freaky means girls that have sex at the drop of a hat. Now I bet all ya know some freaky girls.
COLLABORATOR 2:   Now speaking of that type of girl, all you gotta do is take her to Jackson's Hole and buy 'em a little hamburger, and they're yours for the life! Boom!
COLLABORATOR 1:   That's all. Like all you really have to do is talk to them. Like blah, blah, blah.

Neither Lorna nor Marcia disputed these remarks. Obviously there are young women available to this at-risk population, but there was no indication of a great frequency of sexual encounters, except for the drug users mentioned above. Their attraction may be the drugs, and this point will be discussed in Chapter 8. For many, if not most, in our at-risk population the "freaky girls" are more talked about than encountered, sexually or otherwise. Christopher gives us an example of this when one of my collaborators asked whether his relationships with girls had improved.

CHRISTOPHER: Somewhat, I know a few girls are a little too easy.
     I guess I could do something with 'em if I wanted to, but
     everybody else could too, so that's the problem.
COLLABORATOR: Oh, so you never got into it with them, or you
     never got anybody pregnant or something?
CHRISTOPHER: There's this girl named Dion, but it didn't work
     out. She was an escape from a mental institution. She came in, I
     saw her at Brandeis a few times. Well, she's doing better but
     she would get confused sometimes . . .

It did not seem that Christopher actually had sexual relations with the young woman he described. Yet she was the only girl he described to answer my collaborator's question about his relationships with the opposite sex.

The Girls

Because my collaborators were male, the females interviewed were reluctant to say a great deal about their sexual activities. This is in keeping with Fine's (1988) observations two years previously. The only direct question that came from my collaborators as to whether a particular respondent was sexually active was emphatically answered in the negative. There are more males in the Stay-in-School Partnership than females, and many of the respondents in our data were in the general high school population. Therefore we cannot speculate on female sexual behavior in the at-risk population except to point out that there is obviously a greater pool of males with whom to form relationships. This, we know, changes drastically among this population as the ages increase. By age 30, the available Black females, for example, far outnumber the available Black males.

What can be seen is that the young women had a different view of relationships than did the young men. Of 21 dialogues that involved young women, 15 of them referred to their "boyfriends." Just what the term means to them is arguable, but it could mean anything from the boy she "hangs out" with to a steady lover. By and large, it means more than it does to their male counterparts. One young woman, Lee, after complaining about her parents, spoke of what she does when she cuts school.

> Sometimes I don't really go to school and I hang out with my friends and my boyfriend because they give me that attention that I always wanted to look forward to receiving from my parents and I do not receive.

Boyfriends have an important function for a number of the young women in our dialogues, but the relationships do not always run smoothly. The same collaborator who interviewed Lee later had a dialogue with Ana, a Hispanic student.

COLLABORATOR: How 'bout boy problems? Do you have any boy problems?

ANA: My father don't allow me to go out.

COLLABORATOR: That's why you don't get along?

ANA: That's one reason. He's strict. Cuz his father was real strict with him.

COLLABORATOR: So you don't have a boyfriend.

ANA: No, not anymore, we broke up.

COLLABORATOR: Oh, cuz your father?

ANA: No, my father didn't know. I'm not allowed to date.

COLLABORATOR: Did like that boyfriend help you with any of the problems at home or in school or something? Or did he create problems?

ANA: No, everything was fine at first and then like when we started dating around the fifth month or sixth and we started getting problems. And I was having too many problems, with school, my family, so after seven months we broke up. See he didn't want to break up but I did. I couldn't take it anymore. He was trying. (*Pause.*) He was kind've acting like my father and I don't want that.

COLLABORATOR: Then you had two people being too protective, right?

ANA: I just wanted him to be caring and understanding, and it's like he was real jealous and I couldn't take it.

COLLABORATOR: Oh, that probably really hurt, you know (*pause*), that seven months. That's a very long time. I remember when I went out with a girl for three weeks (*laughter from both*).

At no time did women make contemptuous remarks about men but, of course, they were engaged in dialogues with young men. Lorna and Marcia complained of male behavior, but both took part in the conversation and had each other's support. Had I been able to have young women engage in dialogues with each other, we might have gotten some different data. This is part of what Fine (1988) called "missing discourse."

The women in the dialogues seemed to know what they wanted from relationships and valued them more than did the males. Even if the women establish liaisons with older men, can we assume that the contemptuous attitudes of men disappear as they mature? And is it attitudes like these that contribute to adolescent pregnancies and single-parent families? Before we can answer that question, we must find out what these young people know about sex and contraception.

Contraception

The graphic terms they use to discuss contraception in our dialogues seemed to indicate that many of these young people know quite a bit about it. One of my collaborators brought the subject up with his friend, Syl.

COLLABORATOR: Hey, while we on the subject of birth control, which one do you prefer?
SYL: Let me see, let's say the sponge.
COLLABORATOR: The sponge? What's the sponge?
SYL: Well, it's this little thing that they insert up there and you know it catches the sperm and you know all that good stuff won't get by. It's better than a condom cuz it doesn't pop.
COLLABORATOR: Yeah, that sounds good. I'm like tired of using condoms . . .

I am not sure that my collaborator was having enough sex so that he could actually be tired of using condoms, but his remarks do indicate the attitude of many males in this population who, in spite of the fact that they know about contraceptives, are reluctant to use them. Another collaborator asked a respondent whose stories of his sexual exploits were viewed with some skepticism, whether he ever worried about getting a girl pregnant.

COLLABORATOR: You never worry? Don't tell me that you just screw a girl and you don't worry that you might become a father, and the simple mistake that it might break or whatever.

TONY: Well, sometimes.

COLLABORATOR: Okay, you can't tell me that you don't, cuz everybody thinks so. Even if they say, "I can't have a baby, I gonna
use all these protections and everything." The Pill. Even the
Pill. You use the Pill, you could still get a girl pregnant. It's not
100 percent sure. The only 100 percent sure thing is . . .

TONY: Not doing sex at all.

On the subject of withdrawal as a means of birth control, another
respondent corrected a collaborator:

> Like when a man erects, there's a little bit of fluid and that con-
> tains more millions of sperm. So once you put it in there, that's
> it. It's still gonna go there.

In a conversation on what was good about their dropout-prevention program, one respondent said he liked something called "Teen
Choice," which he said was like sex education.

JAMES: We were testing condoms and all that . . . and different
methods of birth control.

COLLABORATOR: That's great! You actually got up on the table and
tested 'em?

JAMES: No you (*laughing*), c'mon man, she was showing us how to
use 'em. There was like a mannequin and all.

In the conversation with Lorna and Marcia, one of my collaborators, when the conversation turned to AIDS, volunteered that he believed in carrying a condom with him. Adolescent males, of course,
have been carrying condoms in their wallets (often, from wishful
thinking rather than need) ever since condoms became commercially
available. Condoms have long been status symbols to this age group.
In male-to-male dialogues there is much "discourse of desire."

But obviously, many adolescents are sexually active. If our respondents are typical, they have learned a great deal about contraception, and the school should be given credit for that. However, there
is also a negative attitude among males about condoms, if not about
contraception. What is unfortunate is that the respondents who my
collaborators agreed were the most sexually active seemed to have
the most negative attitudes. Again, this may be a result of their drug
use.

ADOLESCENT IDENTITY AND EDUCATION

Erik Erikson (1963) maintains that the major quest of the adolescent is not for sex, but for identity. By *identity* he primarily means a capacity for vocational commitment. He also discusses gender identity and adolescents who doubt their own, but he does not elaborate on this. For Erikson (1963), the need for intimacy comes in young adulthood only *after* the developing person has achieved a sense of identity. Once a person has achieved a sense of identity, she desires to fuse that with the identity of another. But true intimacy cannot be achieved, according to Erikson, without a prior sense of identity. You have to know where you fit into the greater social system before you are ready for a long-term relationship. Falling in love during adolescence is, to Erikson, trying on someone else's identity for size.

The psychological literature on identity focuses on its vocational and sexual aspects and, to a lesser extent, on its political, racial, and ethnic aspects. Harry Stack Sullivan (1953) offers a comprehensive theory of human development that rivals Erikson's (1963) but in which what he calls "the lust dynamism" is the primary force the adolescent has to deal with. How do the words of our respondents fit in with the psychological theory? Does the theory make any sense of the words of the respondents?

There are many more references to sex in our dialogues than there are references to vocational commitment. In the last chapter we saw that it was extremely difficult for these young people to make any vocational choices. Nor did they have the moratorium that college-bound young people do while they make up their minds. Erikson's (1963) notion of moratorium is a "time out" in the growing-up process where a person's psychosocial development catches up with his psychosexual development.

Psychosocial development has to do with where the individual fits into society. Determining this is difficult for the at-risk population. Psychosexual development proceeds in spite of the greater society. If only by default, the lust dynamism, however inadequately these young people deal with it, may become the driving force of their lives. School may be able to help them deal with it, but there is no educational dynamism that rivals that of sex. These young people do not see a link between school and work. Perhaps, however, it would be possible to help them to see a relationship between education and the type of relationships they would like to have.

As part of the Stay-in-School Partnership, we try to pair high school students with mentors drawn from the college population. Sometimes this has a positive effect. In one dialogue one of my collaborators asked a student how coming to the college had changed him.

TOMMY: Changed? Yeah, a lot. In the sense that being with college students, I, like, matured a lot more.
COLLABORATOR: Matured? Mentally or . . .
TOMMY: Both mentally and physically.
COLLABORATOR: You met any college women here?
TOMMY: Actually I have.
COLLABORATOR: How many?
TOMMY: I've only seen one and she really has changed me. She made me a different guy.
COLLABORATOR: What was the old Tommy?
TOMMY: Oh, the old Tommy was kind of crazy. He liked to do all the wild things. Date a lot of wild girls, go out to wild places.
COLLABORATOR (*Laughing*):   Wow, he was a weird kind of person.
TOMMY: Me? The new Tommy, I'm a one-woman man.

The same collaborator got a similar reaction from his friend, Alex, when he asked him if he had changed because of the college program.

ALEX: It has changed me a little. You know, like, I'm involved with older people, people with more sanity, and they teach me good and taught me a bit of responsibility to go to all my classes.
COLLABORATOR: Yeah? You met any women?
ALEX: Yes, yes!
COLLABORATOR: Tell me about her.
ALEX: Tell you about her? Well, she was here and now she's not.
COLLABORATOR: What? She doesn't have any classes?
ALEX: Naw, she's college.

These at-risk students are not terribly different from other people of their age as far as sex is concerned. They, too, with the right motivation, can channel their sexual impulses. The sexual self can become one of many selves rather than the dominant one. There is, moreover, another moderating force on the sexual activity of these young people. That is the fear of AIDS.

AIDS

Apparently, not everyone in our dialogues seemed to know as much about prophylaxis as about contraception in spite of the overlap be-

tween the two. All the students know about AIDS but, while some
have a great fear of the disease, others are convinced that it does not
apply to them. In a dialogue on what pressures young people feel,
Patrice speaks of his fear.

COLLABORATOR: What do [you] mean, pressure?
PATRICE: You just have to deal with everything. Drugs, sex, that
    killer disease, AIDS. You gotta deal with so much things, cuz
    teenagers and sex, I mean that's one of the biggest things now.
    Because teenagers don't know the disease you get from sex and
    have a good time for fifteen minutes, half an hour, and after
    that it's all gone. And then for a little moment of pleasure, I
    could have venereal disease for the rest of my life—and die of
    that. So, you know, I'm not saying that with the first lay that
    you have that you might have it. But a lot of teenagers, they
    don't stay with one girl. They go out and have sex with this girl
    and with that girl; you never know which person was the one
    that gave you AIDS. Let's say I go and have sex with this girl,
    that this girl had sex with these two guys, that these guys had
    sex with those two other girls, and these girls had sex with, you
    know, on a long run like that, you gonna never know who they
    had sex with, and it got passed along until they all had AIDS
    and they don't even know it, ya know what I'm sayin'? Cuz it
    takes five years sometimes to know if you have that disease.
    And then you die. I'm telling you, that's a big problem today.

Syl, on the other hand, the young man who uses drugs and whose
sexual exploits are believed by my collaborators, has different views.

COLLABORATOR: I mean everybody is worried even if they use . . .
    or whatever they use. What do you think about AIDS? That
    you might be too young for AIDS?
SYL: I don't screw sluts.
COLLABORATOR: That doesn't mean anything. I mean if that girl
    you screwed did it with these guys.
SYL: Those guys are homosexual, yeah?

Syl and a number of these young people are convinced that only
male homosexuals get AIDS. As before, there seems to be a link
between such attitudes and the use of drugs. Perhaps drug abusers are
more willing to take risks than others. But drugs will be discussed in a
later chapter; for now we will look at attitudes about other sexual
orientations, especially homosexuality.

ALTERNATIVE SEXUAL ORIENTATIONS

Looking back to Michele Fine's (1988) conclusion that "most students who were gay, bisexual, or lesbian remained closeted, aware of the very real dangers of homophobia," we must remember that she was writing about classroom discussions and interview data. How closeted were gay students in our sample? In our male-to-male dialogues, several gay men volunteered information about their sexual orientation. One of my collaborators engaged a young man, Jackie, in a dialogue about schoolwork.

COLLABORATOR: What are some of the things that you do in school? I mean, let me ask you something. Do you be in good with the teachers and do you do all your work?
JACKIE: Only with the male teachers.
COLLABORATOR: Why only the male teachers? Why not with the female teachers; I mean, they're all teachers. They're all trying to teach you something so you become something in the future.
JACKIE: But the men look good.
COLLABORATOR: So you're what they, you're called homosexual, right?
JACKIE: Well, say "gay."
COLLABORATOR: OK, gay. How's your life as a gay person, in a school? I mean, don't everyone make fun of you and like, don't they treat you different from other people, and don't you feel left out?
JACKIE: Well, see, I show my real self, so they don't say anything to me, but if you act like you're not and you are, then they will.
COLLABORATOR: Ah, OK, yeah, it's true. I very much agree with what you're saying but don't you still think, I mean, deep down inside you think what you're doing is wrong, or do you think it's right, exactly what you do?
JACKIE: Well, you can't say it's wrong, cuz you are what you are.

The dialogue became more graphic in its language and Jackie eventually asked my collaborator if he liked him. When my collaborator emphatically replied in the negative, Jackie ended the dialogue with the words, "Then stop asking me questions like this."

Obviously, Jackie might be a unique individual and the dialogue may not reflect anything like the attitudes of this population toward sexuality or acceptance of what they consider deviant behavior. Another one of my collaborators interviewed two other young men who were known to be homosexual and who give a somewhat differ-ent view. The two young men, Johnny and Barney, are twin brothers on a first-name basis with my collaborator. After introductory re-marks, my collaborator asked them if they had any trouble in school.

JOHNNY: Yeah, we faggots (*laughing*).
COLLABORATOR: When did you find that out?
BARNEY: We just touch each other (*laughing*). We made that mis-take and we got used to it. We kept on doing it, so we got the greatest hormones in the USA.
JOHNNY: No, really, the problem is that one day we were in the same room, see, we had the same room so forget it. We never had a sister before. So we wanted to know, we never had a sis-ter before, why? So one day we went and opened the door on my father and mother, and Barney and me, we found my, you know, having sex. We stared and we stood looking at them. So, you know, it was something weird for me and him.
BARNEY: Yeah, that's true.
JOHNNY: So we went back in the room and we started doing it but we didn't find a hole (*laughing*).

There followed a graphic and explicit description of the two brothers' sexual activity until my collaborator asked when the first incident had happened.

BARNEY: It was, like, around three years ago, you remember the first time? It was great.
JOHNNY: It was exciting, but not like now. Now is like, you know, I can feel it better.
COLLABORATOR: So this is what you guys do when you have prob-lems in school? You relate to each other?
JOHNNY: Hell, yeah! Or we go find other guys.
COLLABORATOR: You guys have problems with school, right, cuz that's why . . .
JOHNNY: No, let me tell you something. There was this social studies teacher, right, and he didn't want to like us cuz he likes girls. So we were after him so he just threw us out. So that's when we started hating him. So that's when they sent us to the principal's office and that's how the trouble started.
COLLABORATOR: Well, talk to me about the problem.
JOHNNY: But really, it's the pressure that we have in school, you know that they don't like gays . . . and we're gays! And we're proud to be gay.
BARNEY: Yeah!

JOHNNY: I love Barney and Barney love me, and we touch each other, we feel each other, and we love each other.

COLLABORATOR: I hope you guys don't start that with me, because I'm not a faggot, OK?

JOHNNY: Well, we know that (*pause*), but you could if you wanted to.

COLLABORATOR: Yeah, it's fun to have AIDS.

JOHNNY: That's the pressure we have. Everybody looks at us and, "Oh you're a faggot, a faggot." And that bothers me; I feel like killing one of 'em. But I'm used to it. But before we were used to it there were problems, problems.

COLLABORATOR: Like what?

JOHNNY: Because the staff used to bother us so many times. Well, we used to walk and a teacher would say, "Look at those two faggots, and I used to get mad, but mad. And Barney too. So you know what we did? After school, we waited for him on the corner and we came for him. And we hit him from all the way behind and he took it to the principal, for which we were suspended from school. So then we went to another school where we went through that, too. So we have the pressure. Today the gays are nothing in this world. But I don't know, getting gay is the best thing you can do . . . love another man. Because sometimes you, what do you say, woman cannot satisfy another man. It feels good, you should try it. I know you feel kind of disgusting but that's the way it is. We can't do nothing about it. We were born this way. We were born this way.

COLLABORATOR: Did you guys ever turn to drugs for your problems?

JOHNNY: Hell, yeah! We used so many drugs, before, so we could change our sexual situation. But no. I've done so many drugs but I still love this guy, and he loves me and we can't, cannot separate. I don't care what people say. I don't care they say, "Oh look, he's a faggot." I don't care no more! Because and [Collaborator's name], you know me since a long time and you know you used to be one of my biggest friends. And I know that since that day you heard that we were gay and you had to stay far away. But that's OK, I understand you like, but one of these days you're gonna understand why we like boys.

COLLABORATOR: Oh, stop! OK, so what kinds of drugs you guys take?

BARNEY: We use dusty angel, crack, horse, marijuana, lions.

Whereas Jackie leads us to believe that homophobia is not a problem, Johnny and Barney convince us otherwise. But the most

serious homophobia they refer to came from teachers. Because of the
animosity they feel from others, their sexual selves are the dominant
selves. Their identities are not formed around a vocational commitment but around their sexual orientations. Jackie appears to have
accepted his; Johnny and Barney are defying the world.

    School has suspended Johnny and Barney (perhaps for good
reason) and transferred them, but has apparently not convinced them
that they need counseling or therapy. Johnny and Barney have been
harassed, betrayed (by my collaborator, from their point of view), and
educationally harmed. They fight back but also resort to drugs. The
wonder of it is that they are still in high school. Gay or straight, it's the
wrong place at the wrong time.

    So the homophobia that Fine (1988) referred to does, indeed,
exist. But these three students were not closeted. Students in general
are aware of a variety of sexual behaviors, and among boys, if not
girls, there is some freedom to discuss them. Overall, however, the
attitudes toward homosexuality among the students sampled seem to
reflect the attitudes of society at large.

THE SEXUAL SELF AND HIGH SCHOOL

The educational concerns of these students pale by comparison to sex
and sexuality. The student self cannot compete with the sexual self.
School has done a good job of imparting sexual information to these
students: They know what sex is; they are acquainted with contraception; they have seen the consequences of AIDS and other sexual
diseases. But the boys appear to lack an understanding of what male–
female relationships can be. In this case, the values of their peer groups
form their notions of relationships.

    Their physical urges and the attitudes of their peers put pressures
on the boys in the dialogues to engage in sexual relations. I suspect that
the actual sexual relationships they become involved in are no greater
or fewer in number than those of adolescent males in other parts of the
nation's population. The sexual behavior of girls cannot be determined
from our data.

    If school could facilitate more conversations like that engaged in
by two of my collaborators and Lorna and Marcia at the beginning of
this chapter, students might gain more mutual understanding and
might be exposed to sexuality as well as sex education. There might
not be the missing discourse of desire that Michele Fine (1988) writes
about. Furthermore, students might see school as a vital place where

they could discuss their concerns while in the process of choosing and preparing for a future career. When a student can integrate his sexual self with his career self, he will become educated.

But from the students' point of view, adolescent-as-sexual-being is a much more dynamic identity, in spite of the stress it creates, than that of adolescent-as-student. This is probably true everywhere, but successful students can channel their sexual drives and subordinate them when necessary to activities that will benefit them in later life. When people are in the wrong place at the wrong time, however, when they have no real reason to be in high school, their sexual selves win by default. If they see no link between school and a career, they might choose only to engage in behaviors that lead to immediate gratification.

3

Self Among Peers

Friends are most often the people our respondents come to for help, rather than to parents, to teachers, to counselors. The most positive, the most admirable behavior that the people in our dialogues exhibited was loyalty to friends. This loyalty was a dominant value alluded to, if not always expressed, in the dialogues. Seeking peer acceptance (by having the right clothes, by having money, by having sex) creates pressures but individual loyalty acts to relieve some of these. This was brought out when one of my collaborators taped a teacher-initiated discussion in a social studies class. Another collaborator in the same class spoke about the role of peers.

> I learned how to be street-smart. I know a lot of people. You know, I know people who sell drugs, you know, I look at them and look at myself and say, "Do you want to be like that?" You know, watch your back, don't let yourself get into so much trouble. And always stay to yourself, and do not trust everybody.

After a comment from the teacher about friends, my collaborator continued.

> The friends I have now is kind of like this. If we don't have no money, they know I don't have no money. They treat me to places and, you know, I treat them. You know, we all stick together.

The self-as-loyal-friend and the self-in-peer-group are obviously related, even though they may sometimes compete. For this reason, both will be covered in this chapter. The self-as-loyal-friend and its implications for the psychology of moral development will be considered first. The self-in-peer-group will then be discussed with particular emphasis on cultural influence and development.

SELF-AS-LOYAL-FRIEND

During a lengthy conversation in school on the subject of drugs, one of my collaborators asked his close friend, Marc, a drug abuser, if he is thinking about his future.

MARC: But I am thinking about my future and I am willing to change; but I need support, especially through my parents, but right now they're not giving me the support I need.

COLLABORATOR: Well, um, that, that is very sad. And I hope that me as your friend you could, like, hang on my shoulder and I'll help you and things like that. I want to ask you a question. . . . If you weren't into drugs, what would you be thinking to be in the future? What would you like to be?

MARC: I would like to be an actor; I would like to be a basketball player . . . and a singer.

COLLABORATOR: But you know to do those things you have to keep clean in those three things. I'm not saying, you know, I'm not saying outer physically, I'm saying inner physically, and mentally also. And I'm not saying this to make you stop or whatever. You could stop when you feel you're ready to. But I'm willing to help you.

MARC: I know I'm doing wrong, but I can't control it. I need it. You know, I need it so much that I can kill, just to get the money to buy drugs. (*Pause.*) Drugs is one of the biggest problems in school.

COLLABORATOR: I know it's a big problem and I want you to know that I hope you know what you're doing and, you know, I was gonna let you talk, let you express your feelings. This is what I'm talkin' here for, so you could have somebody to talk to. (*Pause.*) Anytime you want to talk to me, you could just talk to me.

MARC: I wanta always have the attitude I had before, you know, before I was not using drugs. I know you're a real friend, and I (*pause, crying*).

COLLABORATOR: OK, Marc, you don't, Marc, um (*pause*), you don't have to cry. (*Pause.*) I'm (*pause*), Marc, okay, that's all right, Marc (*pause*), stop crying. (*Pause.*) It's all right, don't worry, I'll be with you. I'll pull you through, don't worry about it. You'll pull through this problem. Marc, all you need is a little

self-confidence, that's it, and with that self-confidence, you
could go anywhere. I mean, just think of this, if you wanta become a basketball player, if you wanta become a singer, if you
wanta become an actor, you need to fix up your life. (*Pause.*)
I'm in back of you. If you fall down, I'll pick you up.

Loyalty as Morality

It is through investigating the self-as-friend that we begin to get
some clues about the moral values of our respondents. What do they
believe in? There is no indication that our respondents hold societal
values in any esteem. Teachers have complained, for instance, that
their students do not value education. Many of our respondents, as we
shall see in Chapter 4, have conflicts with their families and the values
those families represent. There is no mention of church and religious
values. But the dialogues above indicate a strong adherence to the
values of friendship.

Lawrence Kohlberg (1981) offered a now-famous six-stage theory
of moral development. In Kohlberg's view, individuals reason about
and justify moral behavior according to orientations that may change
as they grow older. These orientations are presented as stages, but they
are not necessarily keyed to age. Each succeeding stage, however,
represents a "higher order" of moral reasoning, although two people at
the same stage can make conflicting moral choices. It is how they
make their choices rather than what choices they make that determine
the stage they are in. Kohlberg's stages are summarized below.

Stage 1: Rewards vs. Punishments. Children (and adults) who
function in this stage are concerned with the consequences that may
result from a particular choice. These consequences are determined
by others, such as parents, teachers, other adults, and even peers.
You obey your teacher if you get rewarded for it or if you get punished
for not obeying her. You don't tell lies because you'll get punished
for it.

Stage 2: Self-Interest. Individuals whose moral reasoning is
driven by self-interest are concerned with their own pragmatic and
instrumental needs. You obey your teacher because your teacher will
continue to look upon you favorably, will give you better marks, will
make your school life better. You don't tell lies because you'll eventually get found out anyway, and then your teacher won't believe you
anymore. Kohlberg calls these two stages "preconventional."

Stage 3: Shared Values and Personal Image.   Moral reasoning at this stage proceeds from interpersonal factors. You obey your teacher because he'll be disappointed in you if you don't. You do your homework because good students do their homework. You tell the truth because that's what honest people do. This stage often manifests itself with the coming of adolescence.

On the other hand, the student reasoning on this level may be more concerned with the values of his friends and peers than with the values of teachers. You may tell a lie to keep your friend out of trouble. You may stop doing your homework because homeboys don't do homework; nerds do. The "bad" student, therefore, can be functioning on as high a level of moral reasoning as the "good" student.

Stage 4: Societal Values.   At this stage, the individual is aware of a societal system. You follow school rules, even if odious, because the system would break down if you didn't and no one would be educated. There is an awareness that students are responsible to teachers; teachers are responsible to administrators, etc. Wanting to keep a friend out of trouble might be a noble motive but an ethic of lying might prevent anyone from believing anyone else. Kohlberg calls the third and fourth stages "conventional."

Stages 5 and 6: Postconventional Moral Reasoning.   Appeals to the social contract or to universal moral principles characterize the "principled" stages of moral reasoning. Kohlberg refers to these stages as "postconventional." Researchers in moral reasoning tend not to find great numbers of subjects who function on these levels, and some have suggested that they are not developmental stages. Carol Gilligan (1982) gives a feminist critique of Kohlberg's theory which, she maintains, was based predominantly on data from male subjects. She suggests that a woman's moral development differs from that of a man and these stages, therefore, might not be universal.

For our purposes, we can say that while adolescents certainly can think about, understand, and discuss this type of reasoning, the respondents who make up the data pool of this book seemed to have immediate concerns that overshadowed such discussions, and there was little evidence of reasoning at these stages.

School and Values

A major part of the historical mission of public education in the United States has had to do with the Americanization of immigrant children and the acceptance of societal values. If our students are to accept societal values, they must first see that there is a place for them in society. The socioeconomic concerns discussed in Chapter 1, the problems of disappearing jobs and lack of access to the job network— over which schools have no control—must be made issues of public policy. If there are places in society for our students, it is then a legitimate function of our schools to teach students societal values and to show them the benefits of accepting these values. This is to say, to help them to attain a "higher order" of moral reasoning and to move "up" to Kohlberg's (1981) "conventional" stages.

In the dialogue with Marc, the drug abuser, my collaborator moved Marc because of his friendship. "If you fall down, I'll pick you up." Marc realizes this when he says, "I know you're a real friend." My collaborator is exhibiting the third stage of moral development. He wants to help Marc because that's what friends do; he is interested in the shared values of friendship and the personal image he has of himself as a friend.

A second collaborator, in the class discussion that began this chapter, proudly described himself and his friends with, "If I don't have no money they know I don't have no money. They treat me to places and, you know, I treat them. You know, we all stick together." Again, the choice to help friends is a third-stage choice. But the personal image that my collaborators aspire to is an image to be shared with friends rather than with teachers or parents.

Contrast this with a dialogue that the collaborator who was Marc's friend had with another drug abuser.

COLLABORATOR: Oh man, it's messed up. Do you have lots of
    friends?
FRANCISCO: They're all on crack, too.
COLLABORATOR: You think that they're good friends?
FRANCISCO: Naw, just hang out with them.
COLLABORATOR   Um, so do you think that if maybe you need help,
    that they could help you?
FRANCISCO: No, if they're into crack, how could they help me?
COLLABORATOR: Do you ever worry about having real friends, like
    one time they may help you and, you know, like later in life
    they may help you in something?
FRANCISCO: Yeah, yeah, never thought of it, I don't think.
COLLABORATOR: That's sad, you know, that there's people in the
    world like that.

My collaborator seems to be appealing to the second stage of moral development in Kohlberg's (1981) hierarchy, the stage that involves self-interest. You should have friends because they may be able to help you. But Francisco is unmoved even by this. Drug use, of course, makes the development of moral reasoning difficult, if not impossible. Friendship, however, is generally accepted as a value by most of the respondents in the dialogues.

If young people are to attain higher stages of moral reasoning, they will probably have to do so in terms of friendship rather than in terms of societal values. One should behave in a certain way in order to be a good friend rather than a good citizen. They probably must start with a friendship system before they can understand and appreciate a societal system. Society is an abstraction; friendship is real.

Friends as Counselors

Using his intuition, my collaborator seemed to function very effectively as a counselor in his dialogue with Marc, the drug abuser. He does not judge his friend; he does not push his values onto the other. "And I'm not saying this to make you stop or whatever. You could stop when you feel you're ready to. But I'm willing to help you." My collaborator is, apparently, the only person Marc feels he can talk with about his problem.

The young woman, Lee, whom we met in the last chapter, complained to another of my collaborators that she felt neglected by her parents.

> Fine, they gave me all I needed, but all I really wanted was
> that love from my parents, and I never really received it. . . .
> Sometimes I don't really go to school and I hang out with my
> friends . . . because they give me that attention that I always
> wanted to look forward to receiving from my parents and I do
> not receive.

My collaborator accepted her account without question, without giving her platitudes, such as I'm sure your parents really love you. The dialogue, the same as the one in the last chapter, proceeded as conversation, and my collaborator asked if she had ever thought of leaving home. Lee responded:

> Yeah, well, lots of times I wanted to leave and sometimes just
> end this, end my life. . . . I mean actually yesterday. I was so
> upset. I was so depressed that I felt like my life was useless; I
> was worthless. I was so sad I didn't know what to do really.

And my friends, like I told you . . . they really hang onto me.
Well, you understand they really, they helped me, it was like a
help. And that love and that charm I received from them, you
know, like "Wow, there's no need for me to die."

With the ratio of guidance counselors to students being small, and
counseling often being restricted to course registration, one wonders
whether an organized peer-counseling program might prove effective.
A voluntary program in which students could function as one-on-one
counselors at times and as counselees at other times with other people
might benefit both parties. The people in our dialogues seemed to do
quite well with no training whatsoever. A school might wish to grant
course credit for those who participate in such a program.

Group counseling without teachers or adult counselors might also
work. In the last chapter of this book, I describe an informal group
counseling situation that arose spontaneously in an alternative program. The program was partially built on friendship, something we
educators too often ignore. Many teachers, in fact, fear that personal
friendships in classrooms might work against learning and classroom
management. Friends can reinforce each other to avoid work or to
engage in disruptive and attention-getting behavior. But what if we
had a classroom of friends who all valued what was being taught?
Such a social group will be described later.

SELF-IN-PEER-GROUP

The peer self among many adolescents can override all other selves.
But students in our dialogues seemed to refer to this predominance as
something in the past. Junior high school is, of course, the high point of
this self. Our 16- and 17-year-olds seemed to realize this. In a discussion that was recorded by one of my collaborators in a Stay-in-School
Partnership class on problems of youth, a teacher asked what the word
"influence" meant.

MALE STUDENT 1:   Rub on.
TEACHER: Rub on?
MALE STUDENT 1:   Like somebody you look up to, or something
    like that, or some other people. Like, OK, it's influenced you by
    the way you act. Like, if you see somebody or a bunch of peo-
    ple acting some way, you like that very much the way they're
    acting, and you try to act that way too.

The teacher tried to elicit what kind of people had influence on her students but descriptions were not forthcoming. "Other people" were the only answers.

TEACHER: Not "other people." We said to be specific, what group of people?
MALE STUDENT 2:   Like my cousins, I used to hang out with my cousins a lot. And everything my cousins used to do, I'd do it, cuz I wanted them to know, c'mon, he can do the same thing that we can do. So I would too, even if I didn't like it or something. In a conversation they would say something like . . . I wouldn't like it, but just to make, you know, that they were with me again, so they would call me again and I could hang out with them again. I used to say, "Yeah, that's good," and I would try to make them laugh and everything. But now I don't care. I say that people have to like me the way I am.

The teacher then tried to elicit who were leaders and who were followers. Students admitted to being followers in junior high school. She asked students to recall when a decision was made that a student went along with even when they didn't want to. One girl replied:

Well, sometimes I started doing that, because everybody thought I was like a Goody Two Shoes.

To be a Goody Two Shoes (female) or to be a nerd (male) was to be avoided. These terms might vary from place to place in the country and from time to time, but it indicates the conflict between the self-in-peer-group and two other selves: the self-as-student and self-in-family. Adolescents who can integrate these selves find high school to be the right place at the right time. Those who cannot often have problems. Another student in the same class discussion recalled her junior high school years.

Cuz, when I was young, you know, my friends used to argue with their mothers and everything like that. So you know we [mother and daughter] used to sit and argue. That's when I started messing up in school.

Now that she is no longer "young" she can begin to see the connections between her student self and her family self. It is to be hoped that she can begin to integrate these selves but, as we shall see in Chapter 6, by the time a student begins to make such realizations, she may be a 17-year-old ninth grader with little hope of graduating from high school. But this awareness is, of course, a positive step. The students in these dialogues, whatever difficulties they might have, are those who are still hanging in. Awareness and the will to hang in are surely materials to build with.

Awareness of what influences them varies from student to student and from situation to situation. In the class discussion above, the notion of "forces" was brought up by the teacher.

TEACHER: What are some forces? Do you really think you call your own shots sometimes? Does anybody?

MALE STUDENT 3:   Nobody calls shots on you, nobody can get over on you.

MALE STUDENT 1:   But then again you don't have control over your life. Like, let's say, Uncle Sam wants you, if you gotta go, you gotta go. If you're living in your house, you have to obey your mother and your father, that's one over on you. And school and a job.

Male student 3's remarks are to be admired if he is a self-directed rather than an other-directed person. The influence of peer groups wane as the young person becomes more self-directed and stronger willed. But in spite of such comments, peer-group influence is still dominant, even in senior high school. In the same discussion, the teacher moved from "forces" to "values."

The students volunteered that they valued certain kinds of clothes and spoke of sneakers and jeans. The male students were wearing Nike, Adidas, and Reebok shoes costing from $50 to $75. They preferred $50 Gloria Vanderbilt jeans to $30 Levis. The economic situation of these students would seem to preclude such choices, but one is struck, when walking around their schools, to see the majority wearing expensive sneakers and designer jeans. Their teachers are very much aware of that.

TEACHER: What makes you go out and spend . . . ? You could buy aerobic shoes out of a bin at Pathmark. You don't have to spend $54. You could spend $24. You could buy shoes in John's bargain store for $14.

MALE STUDENT 2:   It's not the same quality; it's not a name brand.

TEACHER: But what's influencing you to make the decision to spend so much money?

FEMALE STUDENT 1:   It's mostly the commercials. You see the girls, the model wearing those nice jeans and they look so nice on her, that you think it's gonna look like that. And you think, "Oh my God, if I get those jeans, I'm gonna look just like her."

MALE STUDENT 2:   Or sometimes they have these car commercials with beautiful girls on the side that come out. It's like, man, if I get that car, I'm gonna get girls just like that, behind the wheel, oooooh.

Although our students give the advertising industry a great deal of credit, it seems they are still influenced by their peer culture in what they wear and how they present themselves to others. How their peers regard them, however, might be one of the few sources of positive reinforcement they get. A student who is failing three out of five subjects, who sees no great future, and who has not yet formed intimate relationships may have to, at least, *look* good to the people who determine his social life.

Peer Culture

This brings us to the question of whether these young people have a separate subculture, deeper than the jeans and running shoes mentioned in the class discussion above, a subculture which competes with the larger culture. Psychologists and anthropologists have coined such phrases as the "culture of childhood" and the media sometimes use such terms as "youth culture." These "cultures" are identified as having their own values, rules, and communication systems. A famous example of this was when child-created lyrics to the music of the popular song "Davy Crockett" were noticed to be widespread in Australia; indeed, several months later, the same lyrics, apparently traveling, virtually unchanged, on some sort of child network, became popular among English children (Opie and Opie, 1959).

Without digressing on just what culture is, let us take a simple dictionary-type definition: the way of life of a society. The attitudes, customs, and language of that society are transmitted by learning. To be part of a culture, or even a subculture, what is transmitted must be adaptive rather than maladaptive. The subculture must somehow function as a survival mechanism. A subculture that transmitted maladaptive values and practices would not last long.

Is there a subculture of the less literate? By this term I mean the varying types of literacy (print, computer, etc.) that people have in varying degrees. I will argue that there is such a culture but that it is *not* based on racial, ethnic, or geographical factors. The respondents in our dialogues were Black and Hispanic; among the Hispanic were represented a number of different ethnic groups, some born in New York and others in tiny towns in the Caribbean. The students I will describe in the last chapter were Whites in relatively small towns in New England.

Although William Julius Wilson's (1987) conclusions in Chapter 1 were based on research among Blacks, everything he says can apply to all those affected by the decline of manufacturing jobs. The students I will discuss in the last chapter, however, were not affected by structural economic changes. What they had in common with the respondents in this urban dropout-prevention program was that they had a small share of the commodity of literacy, their values were mainly formed by and with peers as in the class discussion above, and they were in the wrong places at the wrong times.

These young people had few competencies that the greater society recognizes. One way for that society to shirk responsibility for this is to say they have less "intelligence"; they're not smart enough to succeed in school and learn about the tools of their technology. But a global intelligence that people are born with varying degrees of seems to me a discredited notion. Stephen Jay Gould's (1981) writings have put that matter to rest, and although Arthur Jensen (1969, 1973) keeps producing statistics to support his notion that some racial groups have less of this global quality than others, he has never convinced anyone that his instruments measure anything at all.

Howard Gardner (1983) rejects the notion of intelligence but proposes multiple "intelligences." He defines *an* intelligence as "the ability to solve problems or create products that are valued in one or more cultures" (p. 5). The people in our dialogues are able to solve many problems, for example, counseling peers out of suicide, but few of them have been able to create any products. If school is the only place where they are expected to create products, and if it is the wrong place because the products that can be created in school mostly depend on print literacy, they will not appear to have any intelligences.

If they have a subculture, however, where their solutions and products are valued, they will accept what is conferred or handed down from that culture, more so than from the dominant culture. What is it, then, that is conferred, and is it transmitted differently from what the greater culture transmits? Most important, does what is conferred make for adaptive or maladaptive behaviors? Values are handed down; the ways we think are created in conferment; the way we speak is transmitted. We will see if this subculture is maladaptive.

Values. Conferment, or transmission implies, of course, social construction. In their interactions, these young people create their own values. Selman and Glidden (1987) have stated that "Our research shows very clearly that the cutting edge of children's growth in reciprocity isn't with adults, it's with equals" (p. 20). Coming to school on time, doing homework, staying awake in class are not valued behaviors. Dressing cool, supporting friends, hanging out are. The notion of "face," recognized as one of the most powerful of social forces in Eastern cultures, is dismissed by adults as amounting to nothing among our young people. "Just say no," "Stay in school," they are advised. But if doing something like homework makes you the class nerd, you will not do homework.

But why are what seem to be adaptive behaviors shunned? If society's values are not effectively transmitted by the school, do parents attempt to transmit them? In the next chapter we will see that parents *do* support society's values and try to transmit them. But it is not a transmission with a mutual social construction; it is from above. Moreover, parents of at-risk students are often people who have not been successful in school themselves and do not presume to take over educational functions. They leave education, in all its forms, to the schools and hope for the best.

What we as adults see as adaptive behaviors do not always seem to have a payoff to young people. Our notions of adaptive behaviors, e.g., staying in and doing your homework rather than hanging out with friends, seem to them to be maladaptive. Your peers give you more reinforcement, are your social life, give you knowledge of sexuality and access to sex, counsel you. They are your main access to the job network, no matter how insignificant that may be for many young people. From peers you learn techniques of self-expression and social interaction. Avoiding peers is maladaptive. If there is no future in hanging out, well, there's not much future in school either. And hanging out is much more enjoyable.

If the values you construct with peers are disdained by parents, teachers, and the greater society, you might come to disdain the competing values, if only as a defense. "Here comes the lecture," is a shared response to adult admonitions for most adolescents, but particularly for those who get less positive and more negative reinforcement from those adults. Some psychologists see adolescence as necessarily a rebellious period. If this is so, one would expect those who have less (money, literacy, access to jobs) to be the most rebellious.

Cognition.   Do members of the less literate subculture think differently from those of us in the dominant culture? Piaget and Inhelder (1969) and many developmental psychologists have argued, if not established, that people at different stages of maturity have different ways of thinking. But anthropologists have suggested that different cultures also do. The Tasaday in the Philippines, when first discovered, had no specific concepts for the numbers "four," "five," "six," and so on. They had concepts for "one," "two," "three," and "more than three" (see Nance, 1975).

Teachers often complain that their students have a different concept of time than they do. Some go as far as saying their students have no concept of the future. I suggest that this is a value rather than a cognitive conflict. What their students may be rejecting is the value of delayed gratification in return for future well-being. If they cannot envision a connection between the two, they will not be very willing to delay a good time now.

Jerome Bruner (1986), however, presents an argument about human thought in general that might have some relevance to a discussion of culture. He suggests that there are two distinct modes of thinking, two ways of constructing reality. One of these he calls the paradigmatic or the logico-scientific mode. The other he calls the narrative mode. Each of these, he says, has different operating principles and different criteria of evaluation.

The paradigmatic mode of thought must be systematically learned. It attempts to create a formal system of description and explanation. At a gross level, says Bruner (1986), it deals in general causes and sets up procedures to test for empirical truth. It attempts to use a highly regulated language that is consistent and noncontradictory. Through the centuries, it has developed logic, mathematics, science, and their accompanying technology (abaci, calculating machines, computers, measuring devices) to expand its capabilities.

The paradigmatic mode has its own kind of imagination. This includes seeing connections before they can be proven. This imagination can analyze, develop theory, and make empirical discoveries. Jean Piaget's lifetime work on the growth of thinking in children traces the growth of the paradigmatic mode. He believed that development in the affective domain as well followed, or at least paralleled, that of the cognitive (what we are referring to as the paradigmatic).

The process of schooling seeks to direct the development of the paradigmatic mode. Arithmetic yields to algebra, which yields to calculus in a status system of thinking that leads to more and more abstraction as the child grows older. Subjectivity yields to objectivity as the preferred mode of argument and instruction. Ordered debate is preferred over give-and-take and interaction is formalized: you can't speak until the teacher calls on you.

Whereas the paradigmatic mode tries to transcend the particular, the narrative mode dwells on it. It is concerned with the meaning rather than the truth of statements. Discourse in this mode must be believable. There is a different principle of causality at work in this mode. Bruner (1986) gives two examples which define the word "then," first in the paradigmatic and then in the narrative mode: (1) "if x, then y"; (2) "the king dies and then the queen died." The first "then" implies causality and has one and only one meaning. The second makes us ask if she died of grief, suicide, was she murdered, or was it a coincidence?

Stories children create are likely to be punctuated with "and then," "and then," "and then." Events follow events but do not necessarily imply them. Every teacher knows she will get more attention from her class if she tells a story rather than tries to teach a concept. Even high school students can tell a story with more ease than they can construct an argument. The narrative mode can entertain.

But entertainment is often considered frivolous, and most instruction is carried out in the paradigmatic mode. Actually, there is a spectrum of thought from the paradigmatic to the narrative. Teaching and the mode of thought required to learn in school slides more towards the paradigmatic end of the spectrum; the preferred mode of most students, because it is entertaining and often more meaningful to them, is the narrative. Successful students, who are in the right place at the right time and who identify with the dominant culture, can easily slide along the spectrum or, at least, tolerate the paradigmatic long enough to learn the required material. Those in the less literate culture tend to remain near the narrative end of the spectrum. There are more stories than arguments in our dialogues.

Language. The language of youth is often different from the language of age. There have been many complaints among educators that young people do not speak "standard" English, and many of these educators imply a deficiency in language development. I do not believe this to be the case. Although some of the at-risk population has language deficiencies, so does some of the population that graduates from high school. But it is cultural factors that affect language more than do intellectual factors.

If you grow up speaking Spanish or Vietnamese, your English may be deficient but not necessarily your language. African-Americans have been speaking English for centuries, and it seems foolish to argue that their vernacular implies a deficiency. Eleanor Wilson Orr (1987) attracted a good deal of attention with her book, *Twice As Less: Black English and the Performance of Black Students in Mathematics and Science*. In her book she argued, with secondhand data, that Black children and adolescents did poorly in math because they did not know how to use certain English prepositions correctly.

Orr (1987) conjectured that because of the use of African-American language patterns, Black children tend to misuse eleven prepositions: out of, off, from, between, by, at, to, in, on, up, and down. This misuse, she goes on to say, results in poor performance in mathematics and science. However, I counted 874 uses of these prepositions in all our dialogues and "on" was used incorrectly three times, "in" twice, and "by" only once. A score of 868 to 6 among students identified as at-risk makes one rather skeptical of Orr's argument. It seems to be another theory of basic deficiency that tries to get schools off the hook. If language does interfere with the learning of mathematics, I suggest it is because of teachers' use of such arcane expressions as "twice as less" which few people in any racial group can understand.

The culturally different and preferred mode of thought is a better explanation for low test scores in math than is a language deficit. Howard Gardner (1983), in his theory of multiple intelligences, hypothesizes that there is a logico-mathematical intelligence and a distinctly different linguistic intelligence. By logico-mathematical intelligence he means the phenomenon Piaget investigated as the development of thinking. Bruner seems to be talking about something very similar when he calls the paradigmatic mode logico-scientific. We do not say the Tasaday have a deficit, linguistically or mathematically, because, to them, $3 + 2 = >3$, rather than $3 + 2 = 5$, even though they might not pass a math test.

On the contrary, the Tasaday appeared to do as well as necessary mathematically and linguistically within their culture. The students in our dialogues had no trouble understanding one another in spite of the fact that, from an English teacher's point of view, their language was often atrocious. Pronoun shifts in the middle of a sentence; incomplete sentences being brought to resolution by such interjections as, "ya know what I'm sayin'"; and switching to dialogue in the midst of an explanation, "I was like, . . . 'Wow, there's no need for me to die" are examples of "atrocious" English that effectively communicates.

Many at-risk students appear to be deficient in reading and, especially, in what we call "higher reading skills," e.g., inference. Yet in their speech these people are masters of making and understanding inferences. Face to face, of course, they have the added dimension of body language, yet my collaborators had no trouble reading and understanding the transcripts of the dialogues. In one such dialogue about a young man's relations with his parents, he tells my collaborator, "My father's cool cuz he's fresh. . . . But then he has to, you know, whatever. And then my mother, she's too strict." When I asked my collaborator what these sentences meant, he explained that his friend's father was a bartender and was extremely friendly and knew how to get along with people. It was part of the father's life-style to be "fresh."

There were many examples of inference making in the speech of our respondents. Many are able to create rap poetry on the spot. To fill out a tape (I would not pay my collaborators for less than 20 minutes of material), one concluded with:

> You see I'm five feet four
> I got rhymes galore
> I got rhymes that you never even heard before
> See, I'm a dark-skinned man
> But with a light complexion
> Pull the fly girls in all directions . . .

and 72 more lines of this product valued in his culture which, he assured me, he made up at the time of taping.

Speech, in fact, is central to this culture. In the Stay-in-School Partnership program, we could never get the students to take their lunch during planned activities. They did not want to meet with college mentors over lunch, and even though they were forever complaining about the food in their own schools, they said lunch was the best part of their day. It was the one time during the school day when they could legitimately sit and talk with their friends without outsiders being present.

Culture as Adaptation

Can a competing subculture survive as part of a larger culture while rejecting some of the larger culture's values? More importantly, can the individuals in it survive? I believe that many of those individuals would not survive without it. The peer culture described here helps create what psychoanalyst D. W. Winnicott (1971), called "holding environments." The members of the culture need caring environments

that will help build up their self-esteem, social skills, and self-under-
standing. We will look at such an environment created in a school
program in the last chapter.

There is no economic future in this culture, but it may help them
enter the economic life of the larger culture at least as much as does
school. A friend who can tell you about a job is not much of a network
but the school may not do much better. And, while members of this
culture often reject the values of the encompassing culture, their culture is still not the culture of the streets. Drug abusers and criminals,
we will see, are not admired. Some of the respondents in our dialogues
will, undoubtedly, enter that street culture if they see it as the only
avenue to economic well-being but most will not.

The peer culture can be maladaptive if the peer self is the dominant self, if, for instance, you keep cutting school to hang out, or if you
squander what little bit of money you have on nonessentials. But we
have seen that, as our respondents got older, they began to integrate
their selves-as-loyal-friends with their peer-selves. Francisco, the drug
abuser, had peers but no friends; he was not well served by his
companions. Marc, the other drug abuser, had one of my collaborators
as a friend who might be able yet to help him begin to integrate his
competing selves. And that collaborator realized that the friends he
has "now" are different from his junior high school peers: "You know,
we all stick together."

4

The Family Self

One of my collaborators, in a dialogue with a young woman, Esther, asked what happens when her mother finds out she has cut a class. He wondered if that got her in any "deep" trouble.

ESTHER: She can't say anything to me, I run my own life.
COLLABORATOR: Why? She's your mother, right?
ESTHER: Yeah, she's my mother; she can speak on it but she can't do nothin' about it.
COLLABORATOR: Well, yeah, that's very true, that's very true. So that's a thing you have with your mother, that you could do what you want to?
ESTHER: I do my own thing. It's always like that.

CHILDREN AND THEIR PARENTS

If the subject of family came up, virtually all respondents spoke of friction and parents pressuring them to conform to certain standards. "Oh, I be having a fight with my parents most every day," offered one of the young women in our dialogues. Her attitude did not seem atypical. It may be that in adolescent-to-adolescent dialogues, complaining about parents is common and the population we studied is no different from that of any other adolescent population. The necessary desire to be independent often conflicts with parental strictures.

Adolescent Perceptions

In seeking solutions to poor school performance and dropping out, educators often blame family situations as the cause of these problems. I have heard teachers explain their students' poor performance with such indictments as, "Look at the kinds of families they come from," or "They never read at home," or "Their parents have no control over them." In fact, few teachers have the time or the desire to learn a great deal about the day-to-day family lives of their actual students. Many use a statistical portrait of poor or minority families as a frame of reference and create a mythical "family" for any or all of their students.

This mythical family is often a "broken" family; the head of the household is a female. The family is "broke" as well; probably the majority of the families in the population we studied are officially below the poverty level. The educational level of the parents is often low. What is left out of these descriptions of this mythical family is their struggle and sacrifice. More important, many educators and researchers fail to note that the way children perceive their families is the crucial factor in determining the families' influence. Educators often know little of these perceptions.

Our respondents, in spite of the wide amount of friction reported, recognized the necessity of family support in light of the local economic and housing situation, where the wages of jobs available to them cannot cover rents.

COLLABORATOR: Where would you say that if someone did drop out of school, where would they live?
DONNIE: With their parents.
COLLABORATOR: How about if their parents doesn't want them? How about if their parents, let's say, if you drop out of school, and your parents don't, you know, want their children to drop out of school, and they still do and they throw them out of the house, where do you think they're gonna go?
DONNIE: Well, then, they go back to school. They go back move in with their parents. They don't have a choice.

Is there a discrepancy between Donnie's perceptions and Esther's, or do they simply come from different families with different kinds of family dynamics? Esther does not feel that her mother has any power over her; Donnie and my collaborator see the ultimate power belonging to who controls the roof over the family's head. In a dialogue with one of the young men who had gotten a young woman pregnant and who claimed that he made enough money working so that she could get an abortion, my collaborator brought up the subject of his parents' roles.

COLLABORATOR: Weren't you in trouble with your parents?
BRODERICK: Yeah, but they weren't gonna throw me out of the
    house. They just got mad. And we started fighting.
COLLABORATOR: Did you ask your father for abortion money and,
    you know, he didn't give it to you?
BRODERICK: I asked him and he said, "Naw, you gotta work, cuz
    you decided to do sex, so you know, you gotta be responsible."

Because he knew his parents were not going to throw him out of
the house, Broderick did not feel he was in "trouble." Your parents just
getting mad or giving a lecture is not so terrible. In another dialogue,
the same collaborator asked Brenda about obeying her mother.

COLLABORATOR: Let's say you have a choice about doing some-
    thing with your friends and you think your mother's gonna find
    out, whatever, but let's say you think, "Well, the hell with it, I'd
    rather not have the speech so I'll go and not have my whole
    day frustrated." . . . Or do you feel the other way?
BRENDA: Well, I'll go with my friends. I mean, the speech is just
    like a recording, you know.
COLLABORATOR: I feel sometimes that way, too. I'm gonna have
    my fun and everything and then she's gonna give me the
    speech. It's still not gonna stop me from doing it.

No one in the dialogues mentioned physical punishment. These
people may be too old, their parents may not be so inclined, and, of
course, children and adolescents who are abused often prefer not to
talk of it. It seemed that the only real power the parents had was to
throw a child out of the house. But none of the young women in the
dialogues brought this up. It may be that parents are more reluctant to
use this ultimate act with their daughters than with their sons. Perhaps
because of this, Esther and Brenda had come to realize that their
parents had no real power over them.

To influence their children's behavior, most parents, consciously
or unconsciously, rely on the relationships that have been built up
in the family over the years. But if the peer culture predominates
at adolescence, parents may lose this influence. Parents can compensate for this by using various methods of punishment, such as what
suburban adolescents call "grounding" (not being allowed to socialize
for a certain period). But if socialization is the most important thing
in a child's life, and he chooses to defy his parents, they would have
to be prepared to restrain him physically. Middle-class parents, if

defied, can then take such measures as withholding allowances, cars, trips. If the parents have little themselves, however, they have little to withhold.

The only course left to parents is the verbal one. They can argue, cajole, lecture, or give "the speech." The net result may often be constant friction, an adversarial relationship, guilt, and anger. An extreme description of family friction came from a young man, Roy.

COLLABORATOR: I'm sayin', have you ever tried to stay, like when your mother starts bothering you like that, have you ever tried to stay and talk to her? . . .
ROY: I ain't gonna discuss it . . . if I discuss it, I get madder and madder and then I want to punch her in the face and you can't punch your mother in the face . . .

No, you can't. Even in his anger, Roy recognizes this. Complaints about parents mostly revolved around parental prohibitions which respondents saw as restricting their life-styles and interfering with their independence. Nonetheless, students, with only two exceptions, did not blame their parents for their situations. Marc, the drug abuser we met in the last chapter, and Lee, mentioned in the last two chapters, complained that their parents were not giving them "support" or "love." But in the same dialogue, when my collaborator asked Marc about the connection between parental love and drug abuse, he got a different answer.

COLLABORATOR: Was it just your thought at getting back at them for not loving you as much as you wanted them to?
MARC: Well, none of that . . . my parents has nothing to do with my problems.

And Esther who boasted of her independence above, when asked if she had any family problems replied, "No . . . no, if anything, I cause 'em."

Whether the nature of the dialogues caused our respondents to dwell on the friction with their parents is arguable. But it is reasonable to believe that if a child cuts classes, fails courses, refuses to do homework, exhibits no interest in school, and speaks of no alternatives, there will be friction in the family. To determine whether child behavior causes family friction or vice versa, we must take a sociological look at the family.

Family Ties

At-risk students come from nuclear families, single-parent families, and extended families. I am not aware that any of our respondents came from foster families, but this, of course, is another possibility in the at-risk population in general. Although more and more families in the United States have become homeless in recent years, our respondents were housed and none of them, my collaborators assured me, were housed in shelters or welfare hotels. The only evidence we had of family pathology among our respondents was when one young drug user claimed that his parents were users as well.

The conflicts that our respondents spoke of all seemed to stem from parental desires that their children attend school, do well, and stay off the streets at night. The parents seem to be championing the values of the encompassing society. Even if they themselves may not have performed well in school, they want their children to. Because of where they live, they are probably more aware of problems like drugs than many middle-class parents are, and they seek to protect their children from such problems.

The expensive sneakers and designer jeans referred to in the last chapter are a function of parental support as well as peer culture. They want their children to look nice in school. There are many public schools in the poor neighborhoods that surround City College, and children are seen everywhere. I am always struck by how nice the young children look in September, in the first days of school. Those families on public assistance receive a yearly school-clothing allowance and, apparently, spend it for that purpose. Other families, the majority, accept this value and make sacrifices for their children's appearance.

Only one of our respondents reported any family pressure to quit school and get a job, and that was only because the young man was failing all his courses. In my mother's Irish-Catholic family in Brooklyn, it was understood that daughters were to quit school as soon as they could work, often for the telephone company, although sons might be allowed to attend a vocational high school. In a mill town in Maine, near where I taught high school, many boys stayed in school only until they could go to work for the same mill their fathers did. But jobs for high school dropouts are not plentiful in the cities, and large segments of industry in the rest of the country have closed down.

If the dropout population is not heeding the TV ads urging them to "stay in school," their parents are. Why, then, do teachers complain of a lack of parental support? Perhaps because parents are already doing the best they can. In a suburb of Portland, Maine, where I was a high school special education teacher we set up a state-required parent-teacher meeting, so that we could give a young man some special help. We were going to categorize him as "learning disabled" in order for him to qualify for special services, but all his teachers believed the real problem was that he simply wasn't working very hard. His mother had left work early to make the meeting.

Dedicated teachers and support staff in this meeting were suggesting ways the mother could help her son. Couldn't she check that he did his homework every night? His teachers could call her. Were there any magazines in the home? This single parent, working-class woman, the sole support of her three children, sat there tight-lipped and holding back tears at what probably seemed to her an interrogation. I thought I read in the thought bubble over her head, "Couldn't *you* do these things for me?"

From conversations with her son, I surmised she was worn down from trying to persuade him to do his homework and other such things over the years. She did not relish the thought of coming home from a hard day's work, preparing a meal, and fighting with her oldest. The young man was in the wrong place at the wrong time, and his mother was not able to do anything about that. She could add more pressure to his life in hopes he would respond, but the price would be more pressure for her and more antagonism from him.

But the data do not lead me to believe, for the most part, that adolescents drop out of school because of family friction. Family friction, might be a result of a young person's being in the wrong place at the wrong time, especially when parents value education but do not understand why their child is not doing well in school. There might well be social factors that make it difficult for many adolescents to integrate their selves. Socioeconomic changes might make it difficult for society to integrate its educational system to the world of work as William Julius Wilson (1987) suggests. But, as we have more control over the educational system than we do the economic, we must concentrate on changing the nature of the places we send our children to.

To make such changes we cannot wait until high school. We have seen that by the time many of our respondents got there, they had enough academic handicaps and been retained in grade enough times to make graduation appear impossible. Although the data that this book is based on was collected by and from high school students, we must consider how families and schools interact in the early years.

THE SELF AT THE SCHOOLHOUSE DOOR

The primary self that those well-dressed little children first bring to the schoolhouse door is the self-in-family. The way they giggle and talk with other children, it seems to me, shows a rudimentary self-as-friend and self-in-peer-group. Their eyes, which seem to dart around constantly, taking in everything, indicate a curiosity that a self-as-student can be built on. There is nothing in any of these selves that indicate that they (selves) should compete with one another so that, by adolescence, there is no integrated self.

That the student self fails to develop in many cases will be the subject of Chapter 6. But what is this self that the family creates in the first five years of life, the years before school? A former colleague of mine, a guidance counselor turned administrator, claimed that he could predict in kindergarten who would be high school dropouts. He was quite wrong, of course, except that if such predictions were made known, they might be self-fulfilling prophecies. But on what does one base such predictions?

Erik Erikson (1963) believes that the tasks of the child in the years before school are to develop a sense of trust or confidence in the world, a sense of autonomy for herself, and a sense of initiative with which to interact with the world. Only with these can she then develop a sense of industry in school while she learns the tools of her technology. These first three ingredients of development are learned primarily within and from the family. Would there be anything that has prevented this type of normal development from occurring in certain children?

Trust, to Erikson (1963), is a function of maternal (read "primary caregiver") care. It may be that people in strained socioeconomic circumstances may not, for good reasons, trust the world very much and may communicate this to their children, but Erikson suggests that sensitive care for the baby's needs and a basic trust of the baby are what makes up the baby's sense of trust or confidence. It does not seem likely that good primary care, in this sense, is lacking in proportion to the numbers of people who later drop out of school.

A child who is guided early in life without rigidity to make some basic choices on his own becomes an autonomous adult. He may not develop this autonomy, however, if caregivers doubt or shame him. As with trust, it does not seem possible that whole groups of children are brought up unable to make choices. The adolescents in our dialogues do not seem to lack the desire, at least, for autonomy. And they are certainly not overly rigid, a result of a lack of autonomy.

Initiative in children stems from being active and on the move. If a child is not made to feel guilty for her infantile actions, she will develop initiative. The adolescents in our sample do not appear to be guilt-ridden, and they are not afraid to act on their own. Their parents, apparently, did not stifle any sense of initiative in them.

While some percentage of children beginning school may have deficiencies in their development, there does not seem to be any reason to believe that the self-in-family is not functioning well for large numbers of children. Just as it is not reasonable to believe that very large numbers of children lack the intellectual capacity to complete school, neither is it reasonable to believe that they lack the emotional capacity.

From anthropology we have learned that there is a tremendous variation in family structure and function throughout the world. There are patrilineal and matrilineal families. There are families where wives do not speak to their husbands' relatives or who speak a different language from their husbands. There are extended families, where a number of family groups live under the same roof. There are polygynous families and polyandrous families. There are nuclear families, consisting of father, mother, and children only. There are single-parent families. Each of these represents a cultural adaptation.

But surely there are cultural practices that prove maladaptive as well. Child marriage, for instance, has been practiced for centuries in some cultures, but female children forced into early intercourse have suffered debilitating physical damage. There are those who argue that single-parent families are maladaptive in our culture. Although divorce can be harmful to individuals, the argument loses force as more and more members of the supposedly adaptive middle class find themselves in that position.

What we would want to know is how much the increase in single-parent families has contributed to the school dropout rate. William Julius Wilson (1987) tells us that there was a higher percentage of Black men employed during the Great Depression and more intact Black families than there are now. As we discussed in Chapter 1, the shift away from a manufacturing economy has increased working-class unemployment and, as a result, weakened the family. Much has been written about how much easier it is for a family, Black or White, to receive public assistance if there is no man in the house.

It would be hard to deny that the increase of single-parent families in all ethnic groups has had some impact on the dropout rate. Both the dropout rate and the rise of the single-parent family, however, are effects of the same cause, a structural change in the economy. But from the point of view of the students themselves, the lack of connection between school and work has much more impact on whether they should stay in school or not. There are many divorced parents among the middle class whose children stay in school and attend college.

SINGLE-PARENT AND EXTENDED FAMILIES

Single-parent families adapt in many ways, and one of these ways is to rely on the bonds to their extended families. The single parent may not have to do everything. A number of respondents mentioned aunts or grandmothers who took on some of the functions of parents. One of my collaborators wanted to know where a young woman, Zulma, got her sex education. His awkwardness reflects how difficult the subject is for many people, including parents, to deal with.

COLLABORATOR: I'm gonna ask you another question. Why, when you were growing up, who told you about the changes that were going, I mean, you don't have to answer this question if you don't want to. But, um, like who helped you through like, they say girls go through a lot of changes when they're going to be teenagers, and being teenagers, who told you like, they didn't talk to you or anything like your mother, or was it hard for them, or like your aunt or something?

ZULMA: Well, my aunt was very concerned with me. She really, in fact, I had a cousin that was my age and she took us one day and she talked to us and she, she told us everything straight out.

COLLABORATOR: I really like that because I think that probably helped you a lot and, ah, if you had somebody to, if you had somebody like that every day . . . does your aunt live next to you, around somewhere?

ZULMA: Well, actually no, she doesn't. She lives in Staten Island. And it's really very far, cuz, like, I have to take the ferry and then take a car or a bus that takes me all the way over where she lives. So it's, like, really far.

Zulma's aunt took on a function that many parents would like to avoid. Might it be that Zulma's mother reciprocated and took on functions that her sister might find odious, difficult, or annoying? That Zulma was willing to undergo a long subway–ferry–bus ride to see her aunt demonstrates the importance of other adults in single-parent families. It may be that the extended family makes the single-parent family possible.

Single parents as well as their children need other adults. One such parent once told me that she faced a dilemma whenever her daughter was ill. Should she take the day off from work and stay with her child? Should she let her stay home alone? Should she make her go to school? What she needed at those times, she said, was simply another adult to talk with, "to tell me I'm doing the right thing." A phone call to a mother, grandmother, or sister who might look in on the child sometime during the day can alleviate, if not solve, the dilemma.

When children talk about their families they will talk about their extended families rather than their immediate families. I once asked a ten-year-old boy I was tutoring to describe his family. He listed his mother, his father, his grandfather, and his grandmother, but I was aware that he had not seen his father for years and he saw his grandparents twice a year at most. Respondents in our dialogues from single families all talked about their fathers. "He's in California" or some other place but, in many cases, respondents in single-parent families knew how to contact their fathers. In one of our dialogues, Josh was asked who he discusses his problems with.

I call my father every now and then, if it's guys' stuff. He's in Virginia. My mother gets real emotional, and she's a regular girl, and I don't want to hear any speeches from her. My father will just explain it to me like a man; he won't make such of a big deal out of it. That's what I need sometimes, so I'll call my father.

Extended families also function as refuges for the children. In one dialogue a young man had just arrived at one of our sending schools from Atlanta, Georgia. He had taken a plane and was going to live with his aunt. In another, a young woman was complaining about her father.

CHERRY: I hate my house.
COLLABORATOR: You hate your house? What's the problem?
CHERRY: My father.
COLLABORATOR: OK, what about your father?
CHERRY: We don't get along.
COLLABORATOR: Both of you don't get along? So how can you live in a house when you can't get along with somebody?
CHERRY: I can't, that's the problem. That's why I'm going upstate. See, I wasn't gonna come back to Brandeis at all. . . . And I was going to stay there, but I can't take it in my house, so the only

way is to live upstate with my aunt and go to school up there. I know it's gonna be harder, it's gonna be a change but it's better than living at home.

Three other respondents spoke of either living or planning to live with aunts or grandmothers. This may be unthinkable to the American nuclear family, but there are a number of Polynesian cultures where children often go to live with other family members (frequently the father's brother), when not getting along at home, and the new arrangement might last the whole of childhood (see Mead, 1941, 1961; Malinowski, 1961). In light of the large amount of family friction encountered in our dialogues, it seems a practical solution.

The nuclear family, in fact, might be the exception in the way families are organized around the world. The small size of urban apartments and the often prohibitive cost of large homes outside the cities are economic factors that have weakened the extended family. A college student of mine from Ghana expressed amazement at the housing situation in New York: "You all go home to your little apartments and close and lock the doors every night. You are so isolated."

The single-parent family might also be a consequence of economic factors and social isolation and might indeed be maladaptive. But the reliance on the extended family, even if the members do not live under the same roof, is a positive adaptation to this. The modern extended family creates a network to help educate children, to grant them refuge, to comfort them. Because it is a network rather than a formal organization, however, it may not seem to be a strong bonding force, and the self-in-family may therefore lose dominance over other selves. However, it was there for most of the young people in our dialogues.

A Household

Perhaps a description of the household of one of my collaborators would prove helpful here. I cannot claim that what I will describe is a typical household of an at-risk student among the population studied. I do not believe there is such a typical household. It is a description of how *one* family adapts, and how *one* family contributes to *one* self-in-family. It is a single-parent household.

During the first semester of collecting data with my collaborators, I used to meet them periodically in their sending high school to go over the material, to give them more tapes, and to pay them. They were still engaging in dialogues, however, when the semester ended, and I needed to have a final meeting with them before we went our various ways in summer. I suggested we meet at City College, which was equidistant from all of them, but one invited us to his home and the other two seemed to prefer that.

I parked my car on a street in Harlem composed of rows of stooped two- and three-family houses, commonly called brownstones no matter what the color of the facades. Accompanied by my girl-friend, now my wife, a professor at another university who wanted to meet my collaborators and who was expected, I sought the number of the house. As we approached, we saw a figure who I thought was the young man who had invited us dart into a door at the top of a stoop. On that stoop was the number of the house; when I rang the bell a woman, 35 to 40 years old, came to the door but did not open it.

I assumed the woman was my collaborator's mother, and I believe the young man who darted in when he saw us was indeed my collabo-rator acting under instructions. His mother was to be the gatekeeper of the home. She asked me who I was and seemed suspicious even after my rather complete explanation. Finally, I gestured to her with my eyes and made a slight shrug of my shoulders, as if to say, "C'mon, we're all right." She gestured back with her eyes, opened the door, and led us to her son's room.

My collaborator, age 17, shared the room with his older brother, age 19, and occasionally a friend who had spent the night there. It was an utter mess but no more so than those times when my own sons shared a room at that age. There were phonograph records every-where in old jackets and four huge but worn stereo speakers. Besides the three beds crowded together there was a very used professional console with a turntable for playing records and a myriad of electronic controls. Their equipment seemed professional enough for a radio station, I remarked, but they said they were DJ's. These were the young men I mentioned in Chapter 1 who made money working parties and who had prospects of managing a private club.

The other two collaborators had not arrived yet, so the three young men told us of their dream of the club. My collaborator's older brother and the friend had dropped out of school but were optimistic about their future prospects in music. They wanted to play something for me, but I explained I did not know much about the latest rock or rap. They assured us they could play anything we wanted and my girlfriend suggested Billie Holiday. Sure enough, within seconds, Billie Holiday was singing and at what I thought was the most appropriate volume for the type of music. They were not trying to blow us out of the room, but said that to be good DJ's you had to be able to entertain all kinds of people.

We were in the front room of a two-family house that had been divided into three or more apartments. The paint was peeling in some places, but that was the fault of the landlord. The shades were drawn even though it was daytime because the second-floor room was visible from the street, and the young men did not want their equipment to be seen by potential burglars. Their beds were unmade, but so was mine, I remembered.

My collaborator's mother had left us to ourselves. Because she was home during the day, I assumed that the woman was raising her family by means of public assistance. They all appeared to be physically healthy. I do not know if the boys' father was contributing to the family's support, but my collaborator and, I would guess, the mother knew the man's whereabouts. The man was a Muslim, the religion my collaborator nominally claimed, although no one in the household, I later learned, attended any church or mosque, nor were they associated with any other religious institution.

The young men were being excellent hosts and seemed to want to please my girlfriend. While they were playing more music, my collaborator's mother opened the sliding doors to the room and called him outside. It seemed that a second collaborator had come, but she did not tell this to me. When her son returned, he told me that the other collaborator was reluctant to come in because he felt that he had fallen down on the job; he had not collected many dialogues in the preceding two weeks. My collaborator's mother had been trying to mediate the situation.

I went out and told the young man that his total amount of dialogues was still quite high and that what he had given me was valuable material. More important, I told him that his insights were very helpful in the study. I paid him for what he did turn in and, at that point, my collaborator's mother asked what was going to happen with all the material. I told her that I was going to write an article about it, but that academic journals did not pay any money. Her son then interjected, somewhat annoyingly, that they had been paid for their work (and paid quite well, I thought) but she wanted to know if I would give them any credit. I told her that they would be my co-authors on a possible journal article and, as such, they would get copies.

This woman may not have been very trusting of the world I represented, but seemed soothed when I told her about the co-authorship. She wanted to be sure that her son was getting what he deserved. As head of the family, she was taking her prerogatives. She was the gatekeeper and the protector of her children, even if they did not want her protection at all times.

With the aid of public institutions and of an extended family, she was holding her own family together and very much wanted her younger son to finish high school. She had created a holding environment in which her children could get their lives together even without school. They had a moratorium before they had to earn their own livings. Her predominant self, I would suggest, was self-as-parent, something we will take up in Chapter 5.

Religion

One wonders what other institutions help these families adapt. The family described above had a nominal religion, and we are led to ask what role religion plays in the lives of the at-risk population and their families. Only once did the subject come up in any of our dialogues, and only when a counselor specifically asked my Muslim collaborator his religion. In the class I taught in the Stay-in-School Partnership, I asked who attended church. The only one who answered in the affirmative was a young man whose parents forced him to go every week.

I have been asked, when explaining the paradigm I use in this book of competing selves, why I failed to mention a spiritual-self. The answer is that I did not find it among our respondents. They were not antireligious. Virtually all thought children should attend church, and the majority said that they would encourage any children they might have to attend. They seemed rather to be nonreligious.

This nonreligious stand was curious in light of their ethnic backgrounds. Churches are a very strong force in the Black community, serving a political and social as well as a religious function. Most Hispanics are Catholic and those in New York who are not are usually members of active Pentecostal churches. But among my City College students, most of whom come from backgrounds similar to those of the high school students, only a minority participate in a campus Christian fellowship, the only religious group on campus.

I did hear of a religious presence in some families. The young woman described in the Introduction, who was originally to be one of my collaborators, left the project after her devoutly religious mother threw her out of the house. At this writing, I cannot locate a student to send him some material he wanted because he is no longer living at home. Among other things, he had a religious conflict with his parents and they now do not know where he is. He has also dropped out of school.

Of course, adolescents are not known to be regular churchgoers, but I wonder if what seems to be a relative absence of religion among these at-risk students is a rejection of societal or parental values. I do not know how religious their families are. It may be that less successful portions of the population have fewer social networks in general than others. Wilson's (1987) argument that some people have less access to the job network might only be a symptom of the lack of *any* social network, including a religious one.

The lack of ability to form social networks might, in the end, be a more crucial determinant of low achievement, both economic and educational, than the lack of ability to read and write. Support from extended family and the peer group might not be enough for economic success; indeed, governmental intervention (Public Assistance), the extended family, the peer group, *and* school, in many cases, are not enough. Whether social institutions such as churches or structural changes in the economy would be enough, I cannot say. I will argue later that changes in our educational structure *could* make a difference.

AT RISK IN SCHOOL; AT RISK AT HOME

We have seen that our respondents report a great deal of friction with their families. We have also seen that the problems of these families are the problems of many families. Many of these families seemed to be doing the best they could and their lots probably could not be improved without changes in the economic system. A young man might not want to get a job in the plant where his father works or a young woman in the mill where her mother works, but for many generations that was an option to fall back on. Without such options, education may be the only way up.

Without a secure livelihood, families are strained. Fathers may be encouraged to leave if their families are to be picked up in the public assistance safety net. The single parent—most often a woman with few job prospects but the best of intentions—relies on her extended family for help, but those family members might be in much the same boat. When the children do not achieve in school, they are blamed, and friction and confrontations develop. Adolescents are at risk of having a fight at home and a few are at risk of losing the roof over their heads. They are not at risk with their friends, however.

Those who fail to achieve in school may believe both family and school values to be unrealistic. They do not all realize that, in spite of the friction, their families are their mainstays. They fail to see their families as their major support systems throughout adolescence and, perhaps, through the rest of their lives. As a result, many are not able to integrate their family selves with their peer selves. Their family selves and their school selves cease to develop at some point.

It would seem that their families would support changes in schooling that would improve their children's chances of success. If our respondents could see some value in school or find some meaning for being there, many of their family conflicts might disappear. In spite of their hard lots, parents will often not despair if they can foresee a good life for their children.

5

Self-as-Parent

About 40% of the teenage girls who drop out of school cite pregnancy or parenthood as their reason.

> Karen Pittman
> Children's Defense Fund
> (Lewin, 1988)

A young mother in a dropout-prevention program addressed forcefully the problem of teenage parenthood.

Like cuz I'm a teenage mother, right? And I love my son. I don't care what nobody says. I mean that's me, that's . . . I could have got rid of him . . . but as beautiful as my son is, imagine me killing him. He's a gorgeous child, he's beautiful. I'm not just sayin' that cuz I'm his mother, but he's just a gorgeous baby. I mean, I don't care what people say; I don't care what people say. This is my baby, this is mine. He belongs to me. I have something to love on my own. If something puts me down, if I don't have anyone to talk to or anything, I can go to my son. Even though he can't talk back, he's there for me. You know, when I need him. I want to do all I can. I want to make all the people look stupid. I wanta *be* somebody. I want to have a future so I can have my son . . . everything he needs. He's going to have a good education; he can make good grades. He's not going to deal in crack like all those dumb niggers out there. My son's going to be somebody and his mother's going to be somebody, too. Oh, his father? His father to me is shit. I tell him when he gets to . . . friends, you know and maybe he can because I don't want my son to grow up to know him because he's gonna die anyway; he's living the fast life; he's dealing drugs. I don't want my son to get to know him, for him to get killed in the fast life, you know. That's a . . . nothing. But I got pregnant and I said, "Fuck you." I let him hold him for a while, but he wasn't competent or anything. He wasn't making any effort to show he loved him or he cared about me and his baby. He just lived in the drug life and think he's a crackhead, but I don't give a fuck. He could die today or tomorrow, but I don't care. That is how I feel about him, you know. And as for my son? Everything I got goes to him . . . that's how much I care

about him. I give him the clothes off my back. As long as I . . .
I can look like a bum, I don't give a fuck. But my son look decent. I'm . . . My parents were . . . before he was here, but now
they feel a little better about it. Everyone looks down on teenage mothers. But I tell you one thing, I think teenage mothers
are better than any old person now. If you see a 30-, 24-, 50-,
60-year-old—oh, that's too old—a 35-, 25-year-old mother, they
treat their babies like shit. Teenage mothers take care of their
babies because they know that's all they got in the world today.
That's what I think. That' all I got, that's all I'm living for. I
could kill myself today or tomorrow; I was thinking about that
when I was pregnant, but I said, "This is important. Your son'll
need you or your daughter, whatever you have. They'll still be
yours, a part of you. You can't . . . abortion is killing part of
yourself." Abortion, I'm against abortion. Too much, it's not
even worth it. I love him too much, I care about him. I care
about what's inside of me. I never smoked, I never drunk, I . . .
a good birth. I wanted a healthy baby. Someone I could look
up to, someone that would be all mine. Look what . . . thought.
I'm making money now. I've gotta good job, a babysitter. My
mother and father are behind me all that way. I'm at school.
Most teenagers that have babies drop out of school, you know,
but I'm not like that. . . . I'm gonna go to college, I'm gonna
make money. I'm gonna *be* somebody. And my son is gonna *be*
somebody, too.

This monologue was recorded by another young woman who was
in my high school class in the Stay-in-School Partnership. I had read
the class excerpts from the dialogues gathered by my three major
collaborators and had told them that we lacked female interviewers.
As part of the high school class, I distributed tape recorders and asked
them to collect some dialogues. They were not very successful; doing
something for class credit simply does not motivate this population the
way money does. At any rate, this monologue made everything else
collected by this second group anticlimactic.

PREGNANCY

Teenage pregnancy is considered a social problem by policymakers
and the media. But teenage pregnancy is not quite the same issue as
teenage motherhood. No one knows how many of these pregnancies
are terminated by abortion. In 1970, according to the Children's Defense Fund (1988), a Washington-based advocacy group, there were

68.3 births per 1,000 teenage (age 15–19) girls; in 1985 the rate had declined to 51.3 births per 1,000 or 478,000 babies. (Women under 15 account for over 10,000 babies.) In 1970, however, fewer than one-third of those women were unmarried; in 1985, 58 percent of the teenagers who gave birth were unmarried. Of White unmarried women who deliver babies, 93 percent keep them; of Black women in the same situation, 99 percent keep theirs. White babies, of course, have a better chance of being adopted than do Black babies, and there may be more pressure on unmarried White women to give theirs up.

Why do unmarried teenagers become pregnant? I do not think there is a single answer to this question. Lust, love, loneliness, rebelliousness, desire for affection, desire to become a mother, the quest for identity, pressure from partner, peer pressure, lack of knowledge of birth control, accidents, cultural factors, the promise of public assistance, and social biology have all been offered as possible reasons. Let us briefly consider these possibilities, with no expectation of arriving at an answer, in examining the monologue that began this chapter.

Lust, love, loneliness, rebelliousness, and desire for affection are individual psychological factors that explain why people—teenagers as well as adults—have sex, but alone these factors do not adequately explain pregnancy. Few unmarried teenagers consciously set out to become pregnant. There may be unconscious factors, of course, but conclusions on such factors can only be determined on a case-by-case basis. In the mother's monologue above, the desire for her child's affection was a strong impetus to continue her pregnancy.

Once pregnant, the young woman came to terms with her desire to become a mother. She wanted a healthy baby that would be all hers. After the birth, the baby seems to have given her an identity, a defined purpose in a social setting. Her self-as-parent became her dominant self. But, to reiterate, this did not occur until *after* the birth. It does not seem likely that she would have anticipated this new sense of self before she became pregnant.

There was undoubtedly pressure from her partner to engage in sex, but the young woman mentions no such pressure from him to have a baby. Another interpersonal factor would be peer pressure. Did she know any other teenage mothers who spoke so powerfully and movingly about their children as she did? We do not know, and neither do we know whether the thoughts she so eloquently expresses will influence other young women. Judging from the importance of the peer self that was outlined in Chapter 3, friends may indeed be a contributing factor.

But do these motivations occur only after pregnancy? How many pregnancies result from a lack of knowledge of birth control or from "accidents"? Young people in the age bracket of those in our dialogues in New York City are, in general, knowledgeable about birth control. This may not be the case in all other parts of the country. Young men may be reluctant to use contraceptives, but diaphragms and the Pill are more the woman's choice. We wonder what is happening in a case such as that described in *In a Different Voice: Psychological Theory and Woman's Development* (Gilligan, 1982), when a young woman explains that she became pregnant when she "just" left her diaphragm "in the drawer." That was, apparently, no accident.

Are there cultural factors that encourage young women to become pregnant? While only 5.13 percent of teenagers (age 15–19) become mothers each year, the rate can vary drastically from place to place (National Center for Health Statistics; see Lewin, 1988). According to one account, one-fourth of Los Angeles's Jordan High School's 1,000 girls have babies each year (Read, 1988). They may be influenced by their peers, and there may be financial support available to mothers, but their parents certainly do not encourage them.

But if their mothers or their sisters are supported by public assistance, they might also choose that road, in spite of any admonitions they hear from those very people. Cultures, even subcultures, seek to sustain themselves. It may be that the at-risk student with little promise of success in the greater society becomes a part of an underclass culture, and early pregnancy may be an adaptive behavior for members of this culture. A child can give an identity and economic support, albeit meager; also, parents in this culture, in spite of their admonitions, tend to help their unmarried daughters with their babies.

The data of this study do not support such an argument but, if early motherhood is a function of culture, it is probably determined unconsciously. Another possibility, not determined consciously, is a social-biological factor. The sociobiologist says that biological factors, for the most part, determine what society does. The average age of first pregnancy in most species probably does not change appreciably over time. If the average age of first pregnancy in, let us say, wolves is 13 months, it was probably also 13 months 25,000 years ago. The wolf is on a biological timetable determined by the life span of the species. The species is genetically programmed to reproduce itself.

With humans, of course, it is more complicated. Age of first pregnancy varies with the age of puberty and we know that the age of puberty varies with, among other factors, nutrition. The age of puberty in the United States has been lowered in the last 50 years. A sociobiologist might argue that the mean number of years between puberty and first pregnancy remains relatively constant, however.

Statistically, these pregnancies will be distributed on either side of this mean. A certain percentage of individual pregnancies, therefore, will occur in women as young as 13, 14, and 15 years old. A five-percent teenage-motherhood rate may be totally expected.

I am not necessarily advocating the sociobiologist perspective, but we obviously cannot eradicate teenage pregnancy. According to the Children's Defense Fund (1988), of the 9 million women aged 15 to 19 in 1985, 47 percent were sexually active; of those, 49 percent did not use contraception; of the 47 percent, 23 percent became pregnant; of those, 48 percent gave birth. With education and with easier access to birth control and abortion, we can, if we wish, lower those rates, but we cannot lower them indefinitely. What we can do is make schools the right place to be at the time of motherhood.

MOTHERS AS STUDENTS

When I started my teaching career, girls who became pregnant were obliged to leave school. Usually, they went to special homes where they could have their babies and, if they wished, give them up for adoption. Enlightened school districts might let the young woman return to classes, but this was rare. There are still many districts where, even though it might be legally permissible to return, social factors make reentry impossible. When reentry is blocked—considering that many, if not most, of these young women lack any job skills—a problem for society is created. Teenage motherhood, I believe, need *not* be a problem as long as measures are taken to ensure the health of both the mother and child.

But educators are not public health professionals, and they must ask themselves if there is a link between school factors and pregnancy. Much has been written about early pregnancy as a function of race. The Children's Defense Fund (1988), however, found that poverty and poor school performance were more salient variables in the teenage pregnancy equation than was race. When pregnancy data are adjusted to reflect family income and academic performance, there is no difference between White, Black, and Hispanic adolescents.

The Children's Defense Fund (1988) reports that whether White, Black, or Hispanic, one out of every five 16- to 19-year-old women from poor families and with below-average school performance was a teenage mother in 1981. Furthermore, whether White, Black, or Hispanic, only three to five percent of all 16- to 19-year-old women from families above the poverty line and with above-average school perfor-

mance were teenage mothers in the same year. Poor school performance has long been recognized to be a function of poverty. So, while
poor school performance cannot be said to be a causal factor in
adolescent pregnancy, there is a relationship.

Schools alone cannot solve the social problem created by mothers
unable to support themselves. Obviously, if a mother is to return to
school, there must be some facility providing day care for her children.
A few schools do have their own day-care facilities, but budget con-
straints make such programs difficult. Policymakers must realize that
adequate day care is the first step to moderate the social effects of
teenage motherhood. If you cannot get teenagers to school, or other educational facility, you cannot give them marketable skills. If you cannot
help them take care of their children, you will not get them to school.

But the day-care problem aside, what must schools do to alleviate
the problem? In the last chapter of this book, I will address possible
solutions to the dropout problem in general. Here, I would like to
discuss what values society and, necessarily, schools must advocate
regarding motherhood. Schools can teach about but cannot regulate
sexual behavior, for the obvious reason that this behavior, for the most
part, does not occur in school. School, therefore, should not punish
girls for getting pregnant by throwing them out or by any other means.
Motherhood should never be equated with something bad, and there
should never be a stigma attached to it.

The young mother whose monologue began this chapter speaks to
a stigma that she feels. "Everyone looks down on teenage mothers,"
she says. Although she feels that her parents help her, she does not
mention any other cultural support. The stigma she feels must have
come from parents, church, school, the media, and/or peers. One
might argue that the stigma has helped motivate her in her heroic
efforts to "be" somebody, but surely her life would be easier without
it. In any case, if she is to continue her education, school should be the
last place to promote such a stigma.

Could anyone have argued that motherhood would be a bad thing
for this young woman? Would it have been bad when she was the
pregnant girlfriend of a drug dealer? Would it have been bad before
that, when she was failing in school and sleeping with a drug dealer?
Would it have been bad before that, when she was just failing in school
and seeing no prospects for success? I am not suggesting that anyone
should have counseled her to have a baby, but imploring her to study
harder to ensure future success and preaching sexual abstinence to
avoid the stigma of pregnancy and the horror of venereal disease
obviously did not help.

It is motherhood, and perhaps only motherhood, that is enabling this young woman to turn her life around. In the best of all possible worlds, or rather the ideal world for my culture, I would have preferred her to succeed in school, to remain sexually abstinent at least a few years longer, to embark on a career, and then to marry a man in similar circumstances and have children. But this is not the best of all possible worlds, and my preferences can have no bearing on her life. She is ordering the events in her life differently than I would order them for her, but it may be the only order that will work for her.

She has a self-as-parent and a self-in-family. She is trying to integrate these selves with a self-as-student. I do not know what she is doing about her sexual self but she has a peer self, I am told, that does not conflict with any of the others. Her goal to "be" somebody will, it is to be hoped, lead to a career self. I fear, however, that she will not be able to integrate the selves that she has developed with her self-as-student. Although she is in an admirable dropout-prevention program, she may not be able to develop the kind of skills that will ensure success.

Another fear stems again from data generated by the Children's Defense Fund (1988). Forty-three percent of the teenagers who gave birth, the data suggest, will have a second baby within three years. Two children can make it extremely difficult for a woman to complete her education. If we can assume increased motivation for academic and financial success, as our young mother demonstrates, this would be an appropriate time to reinforce her knowledge of family planning.

Her program may indeed help her to graduate from high school, and her effort will cause her basic skills to improve, but there are few vocational subjects available to her. She may have to continue her education after high school. With her drive she may well be able to do this; nonetheless, it will mean years and years of schooling slowed down by part-time work. With fewer skills she will have to work harder than her middle-class peers and reorder the events of her life to conform to middle-class values. Ultimately, she may not choose to do this.

The young woman claims to have a "good job" as a babysitter. By "good job," does she mean that she enjoys the work or that she has a good salary? She cannot be well paid, but the only other job, in all likelihood, that is available to her is to work in a fast-food restaurant. If she enjoys taking care of children, perhaps she will become a teacher. But the "good" jobs available to her might become counterproductive in her eyes, if she has to spend too many hours away from her own child to earn enough money for necessities. And the education available to her might also seem counterproductive if the number of hours spent in school for the marketable job skills received also appears too high. A program that combines earning with learning is needed for these young mothers.

YOUNG FATHERS

The general belief that the unmarried mother, her family, and social welfare agencies bear the brunt of raising her children without any help from fathers is not an implied value, but is based on the realities of the circumstances of teenage parenthood. The young mother in this chapter does not want anything to do with the father of her child. In this choice, she is right. Does she want her child to be supported by drug money? Does she want this drug dealer to be a model for her son?

As young women tend to become involved with men slightly older than they are, the fathers of their babies may well have finished their education for one reason or another. If they have dropped out of school, they may not be in any kind of position to support their children. Even if they have graduated, they simply might not be making enough money to support even themselves. Marriage, once the ideal solution to the problem of teenage motherhood, is not a solution at all. Few of these young fathers are emotionally or financially prepared to start their own families.

This is even more the case for those fathers still in school. The best that can be expected from those young men is a token support payment coming from a low-paying, part-time job. If these fathers are to ever become providers, they must continue their education. But what values should society and school advocate for young men regarding fatherhood? If motherhood should never be considered a bad thing, even if the girl is unmarried, what of fatherhood?

The case of young men, unfortunately, is different from that of young women. Even if we could remove the stigma from unmarried pregnancy, the mother still has the burden of raising her child. Most young fathers escape this, largely because of a socially recognized incompetence. Irresponsibility in young men is a socially constructed reality. We correctly believe that most are unprepared to earn enough to support a family, but we label this unpreparedness as irresponsibility. And it is probably this socially constructed irresponsibility that contributes to two male attitudes expressed in Chapter 2: getting a girl pregnant as a rite of passage and contempt for women.

Fatherhood does not turn the lives of young men around as it did that of the young woman whose monologue began this chapter. A young man's self-as-parent does not ordinarily develop during his adolescent years, even if he becomes a father. Getting a girl pregnant might gain him status among his friends and might add to the peer self. Adults tell him that getting a girl pregnant is wrong but give him no means to rectify the situation.

As a society, we have not made up our minds as to what we expect of teenage fathers. This ambivalent attitude, coupled with the contempt that women such as our young mother have for their partners, might preclude many young men from ever assuming the sustained responsibilities of fatherhood. Schools do not educate young men to be fathers. They do not educate young women to be mothers either, but pregnancy and birth themselves are experiences that bond a mother to her child.

The best that schools can do is provide the best possible education so that young men can ultimately become providers, at least in the financial sense. Schools are equipped to teach basic skills; they can be equipped to teach more vocational skills. Schools alone, however, cannot teach values like parental responsibility, which includes the responsibility *not* to become a parent. Moreover, they can welcome teenage mothers and fathers so they can complete their educations, thus linking education with the world of work.

THE RIGHT TIME

This book opened with the idea that many young people are in the wrong place (high school) at the wrong time (adolescence). So far, the criticisms of formal education have concentrated on the place and have not spoken to the time. But we have seen that our determined teenage mother and many others like her are ordering the events of their lives differently than most other people in our culture. We might ask, then, whether they can receive their education at another time that might be more opportune for them.

Adolescence as a life stage is a socially constructed concept. There are cultures that recognize no such stage. Individuals in such cultures might proceed from childhood to rite-of-passage to adulthood. Women in similar cultures might go from childhood to puberty to adulthood. Because it takes a long time to learn the complex technology of our world, we have created a moratorium for our young people. (See Erikson's [1963] definition in Chapter 3.) At puberty we are physically capable of being parents, but an industrial society assigns us no social role at that age. The moratorium of adolescence—and beyond, in the case of those who attend college and graduate school—allows us to find an identity, to decide on a career, to integrate our selves. Adult opinion on how to deal with one's sexuality during this period runs from abstinence to contraception.

One hundred years ago in our culture most people went to school until they found a livelihood. If a young man impregnated a girl he was expected to quit school, marry, and support her and his offspring. But there was work in factories, there was day labor, there were 160 free acres of land in the West for the working. Adolescence, such as it was, ended at parenthood if not before. I do not mean to suggest that this was a golden age, but socioeconomic conditions made for a different ordering of the events in one's life.

The middle-class ideal today for life events is (1) schooling, (2) career establishment, (3) marriage, and (4) children. Sexual initiation can occur in any of the first three periods and, in recent years, has been occurring earlier. Traditionally, young men's sexual initiations were thought to occur before those of young women, but this may no longer be the case.

Very recently, the life-event intervals of upwardly mobile people have changed. Numbers of women have postponed having children while they prosper in their careers. Schooling can reoccur at later ages, as people make career changes and further postpone having children. Career women who have postponed marriage, though, find themselves part of a disadvantageous male–female ratio in their mid-thirties. We see numbers of "last chance" pregnancies among women in their late thirties. With divorce, the four life events mentioned above have been extended to six or eight, counting recurring marriages and children.

The culture of the middle class, then, can influence women to delay pregnancy, among other things, until their late thirties. Perhaps the culture of other classes influences women to move up their pregnancies to their teenage years. Compared to the White population, Black males are more likely to be in prison, the military, or die at an early age. The Black woman who postpones marriage and pregnancy till her mid-thirties finds that there are a hundred available Black women for every fifty available Black men. It might be culturally advantageous for her to have her children early.

It is, of course, difficult to argue that the aforementioned statistics are on the minds of individuals who choose to have their children early. And unmarried motherhood is certainly not restricted to Blacks.

In *The State of Black America*, Andrew Billingsly (1987) points out that the pregnancy rate of unmarried White teenagers in America is higher than that of any other western industrialized nation. Whatever factors are operating, we cannot expect that all women will follow the traditional order of life events.

For a certain percentage of the population, many of whom are in the at-risk category in school, the order of life events might be (1) schooling, (2) children, (3) schooling, (4) career establishment, (5) marriage, (6) children. It also may be that marriage and/or more children will not be part of their lives. With this order of life events, the opportunities for schooling (timewise) might have to be changed. This change is already occurring, as indicated by the rise in adult education and the advancing age of college students. Unfortunately, when public expenditures are cut, adult education is often the first item to go.

If pre- and postnatal child care is the first choice of policymakers to alleviate the problems associated with teenage pregnancy, adult education must be the second. Without further education, career establishment may never happen. Young adulthood (or old adulthood, for that matter) rather than adolescence might be the right time for some people to learn necessary job skills. We must have the right places available at all times.

But education for such people as the young woman who wants to "be" someone might take a different form than that of the comprehensive high school. She may graduate from high school but be no further along in the area of career choice. Students in the dropout-prevention program in her school do not usually take vocational subjects. Most are playing catch-up with basic skills. After a year in the program, students still in school return to the mainstream. If they intend to graduate, they must take the required subjects, which they might have previously failed, and not have time for the few vocational subjects that are offered.

Moreover, this woman whose time is taken up caring for someone else's children, raising her own son, and getting through school cannot be expected to take up the traditional life-style of a student. Does a woman who has delivered a child and has responsibility for others need to have permission to go to the girls' room? Does she need a pass to be out in the halls during classes? Will she have to bring a note from her mother if she is absent? As a former high school teacher, I realize that there are very good reasons for these regulations, but I am not sure they create an appropriate environment for this young woman.

If we do not change the time of her education, we must change the nature of the place she is in. It would seem that the time is ripe for

the woman of the above monologue to continue her education; she
may be more motivated to learn than at any time previously. But, she
still might be in the wrong place at the right time.

THE DOWNSIDE

Our discussion of teenage pregnancy has been from an educational, a
psychological, and, to some extent, from a sociological point of view.
But the young mother in the dropout-prevention program introduced
another factor when she said, "I wanted to have a healthy baby."
Before concluding this chapter, I would like to take a brief look at the
public health aspects of early motherhood and investigate the young
mother's claim that teenage mothers are better parents than others.

In their fascinating but disquieting book, *Women in the World: An
International Atlas*, Joni Seager and Ann Olson (1986) report that,
worldwide, official marital status has little influence on women's childbearing experiences. In the United States, in 1984, we averaged 210
out-of-wedlock births per 1,000 births, according to the National Center for Health Statistics (cited by Seager and Olson, 1986). Youth,
however, has a great influence on women's childbearing experiences.
Seager and Olson (1986) conclude that, worldwide, high death rates
are associated with early marriage and childbearing and with low
levels of education for women.

The National Center for Health Statistics (Seager and Olson,
1986) reported that, in 1985, the infant mortality rate in this country
was 10.6 deaths per 1,000 births, a rate higher than that of most
western industrialized nations and nineteenth in the world. The rate
among all minorities is double that figure, although infant death rates
attributable to unpreventable causes was virtually the same for all
races. Clearly then, prevention of infant mortality is a function of pre-
and postnatal care. The maternal mortality rate (deaths due to pregnancy) reflects similar imbalances, with the minority rate being more
than twice as high as the overall rate. Since there does not appear to be
a biological difference in the races, we can attribute this difference to
inadequate care.

One group of pregnant women likely to receive less care is the
young. Because of the stigma that our mother speaks of, many pregnant teenagers will hide their condition as long as possible and receive
no prenatal care during that time. Our respondents knew a good deal
about birth control, but could only learn about managing a pregnancy
by observation of friends and relatives. Because of lack of care and

knowledge, teenage mothers have a greater risk of complications during pregnancy and birth.

This lack of knowledge extends to lack of knowledge of how to parent. The admirable qualities of our young mother might not be universal. Apparently, she knows enough about child care to be trusted as a regular babysitter, but her statement about teenagers being better mothers cannot be verified. There is no reason to believe that teenagers make better mothers, even if their babies are "all they got in the world today." We cannot say they are not so good, but we can certainly say that they are not so prepared.

TEENAGE PARENTHOOD

I have argued that teenage parenthood is not a bad thing in itself. A certain number of women will have their children in their teenage years whether they are married or not, whether they are in school or not. If women can bear children between the ages of 13 and 50, it is likely that some children will be born at the extreme ends of the span. We can probably decrease the number of children born to young women depending on how Draconian we choose to be, but we will not eradicate it. The rate *is* decreasing, however.

Current social policies have made teenage parenthood a problem. Poverty and lack of vocational training make it impossible for most teenagers to support any children they may have. That there is little free education for people over 20, and that there is an inadequate amount of day care for children, makes it difficult for mothers ever to be able to be breadwinners. For the same reasons, it is unrealistic to hold teenage fathers accountable for child support.

I think we must accept that in a heterogeneous and multicultural society such as ours, some people are going to order the important events of their lives differently than others. And we should be open to the possibility that a teenage or out-of-wedlock birth might be a good thing for some people. Human development proceeds before, during, and after our childbearing years.

An enlightened child support system, as exists in some Scandinavian and other European countries, government-sponsored day care, and free education for people of all ages might not eliminate teenage parents, but it would eliminate many of the so-called problems. It is interesting to note, however, that in countries that have made these reforms, the adolescent pregnancy rate is lower than ours. Good pre- and postnatal care should go without saying but, alas, we lag behind most other industrialized nations in these areas. Pregnant teenagers probably get less of this care than others.

But this book is about educating the at-risk student. Efforts at sex education must be continued in our schools and be expanded to those schools that do not presently have it. Students must be made aware of both prophylaxis and family planning, and school is the only place where we can be sure this is accomplished. No stigma should be attached to pregnancy, and young men must come to realize that someone else may have to pay for the consequences of their actions. Teachers might consider, in discussing moral choices, appealing to the morality of friendship and personal loyalty, as was suggested in Chapter 3.

Pregnant women should be encouraged to continue their education before and after the birth of their child, but this education should be more closely linked with the world of work and, if possible, with programs of paid work with academic credit. The at-risk student who becomes pregnant is still at risk, even if she becomes highly motivated because of her newly found self-as-parent. The student self, which we will talk about in the next chapter, must be integrated with the self-as-parent. In order to do this, the young mother may need a different kind of place in which to learn, in Erikson's words (1963), "the tools of" her "technology" (p. 259) and her role in the greater society. In addition, she may need a different, and perhaps extended, time in which to accomplish these things.

6

The Student Self

In trying to find out why people drop out of school, one of my collaborators, Ron, interviewed the other two.

RON: Why do you think someone drops out of school?

GEORGE: I think people drop out of school cuz of the pressure that school brings them. Like, sometimes the teacher might get on the back of a student so much that the student doesn't want to do the work. . . . And then that passes and he says, "I'm gonna start doing good. . . ." Then he's not doing as good as he's supposed to and when he sees his grade, he's, "you mean I'm doin' all that for nothin'? I'd rather not come to school."

RON: Okay, all right.

RASHEED: I think kids drop out of school because they gettin' too old to be in high school. And I think they got, like, they think it's time to get a responsibility and to get a job and stuff. And, like George says, sometimes the teachers, you know, tell you to drop out, knowing that you might not graduate anyway.

RON: How does a teacher tell you to drop out?

RASHEED: No, they recommend you take the GED program sometimes. Like, some kids just say, "Why don't you just take the GED. Just get it over with." Then, job or something.

RON: You talked about a kid being too old. Why is a kid too old?

RASHEED: Cuz he got left back too many times.

SCHOOL VS. SELF

This conversation gives us four reasons why at-risk students react negatively to school: (1) the teacher's "getting on your back" so you don't want to do the work, (2) pressure to obtain good grades, (3) the need to start a career by a certain age, and (4) even encouragement to drop out. I will address the first reason in greater detail in the next chapter, after discussing the other three reasons here.

Grading as a Economic System

Martin Covington and Richard Beery (1976) remind us of the obvious but sobering fact that there are more students who aspire to good grades than there are good grades. Grading often becomes a competitive system, where one student succeeds at the expense of another. The child who is slowly groping for an answer to his teacher's question can be surrounded by a flock of flapping hands, all vying for attention. Others have the answer that he lacks. The child who is then called upon to correct him gets her reward because of his failure.

Covington and Beery (1976) report that in the early part of this century, Daniel Starch introduced the normal—or what we call the bell-shaped—curve and the ABCDF system to school grading. By using this probability-based system, we guarantee that there will be few high grades even though a classroom is almost never a normally distributed group where the bell-shaped curve applies. A teacher who gives all A's is likely to be questioned by his superiors no matter what the ability level of his classes might be.

This competitive system appears to mirror the larger economic system, with its pressures and lack of rewards for the population from which our respondents are drawn. Many studies, of course, have shown that there is a correlation between school success and family income. If school is a preparation for life, as some think, does lack of success in the former, with its accompanying fear of continued failure, boredom, acting out, and declining motivation, prepare young people to endure a similar life-style as adults?

Few of the adults who teach these young people have any idea of what this lack of success means to them. Most teachers have been successful in school; they do not always understand how a report card might be a periodic dread. Nor do they understand how failure often becomes a constant part of the school lives of many students.

RICH: Last marking period I failed gym, typing, and government.
FRANKIE: I failed all my subjects.
COLLABORATOR: You only failed math, right?
MARVIN: Yeah, math.

By the time they get to high school, students used to failure often disparage school and teachers. The conversation with Marvin continues:

COLLABORATOR: Why [did Marvin fail math]?
MARVIN: Why? Because I don't like him and he thinks I'm a joke.
So I make believe I'm a joke.

I know a principal in the state of Washington who peruses the college transcripts of his prospective teachers. He looks for teachers who have an F on their transcript so they know how it feels. He does not believe that students are jokes, even though they might joke about failure. Young people making light of their lack of success in school can be misinterpreted by teachers as not caring whether they pass or fail. The people in our dialogues *wanted* to pass; most had volunteered for their dropout-prevention programs.

They do not want to fail just as they do not want to be poor. Students used to failure, therefore, *cannot* bring themselves to link school with the future world of work. One's student self comes into conflict with one's career self. They can keep trying; they can reject school. If school is a mandatory credential to a legitimate career, they can attempt an illegitimate one. My collaborators engaged in dialogue with a few people who had dropped out, and with one young man we will meet in Chapter 8 who is engaged in other than legal activities; but, to their credit, most of the respondents are still trying, still hanging in, even though they may be in the wrong place.

Retention in Grade

One of my collaborators was retained in grade twice; he is two years behind the people he started school with. Many in the population have been retained at least once. The roots of the dropout problem may, therefore, begin long before high school, and promotion at that level has to do with the cut-and-dried system of how many credits have been earned. A 17-year-old who has only enough credits to be a ninth grader may see little chance of graduating. With little hope, anyone with common sense might avoid failure by refusing to participate in the system.

In my opinion, it is extremely difficult for a student who has been retained in grade twice ever to graduate from high school. In my twenty years' experience in schools, I did not find that the majority of children retained in grade did any better the second time around. Those who criticize schools for "pushing students through" have not presented a practical alternative. If the place called school is not good for a particular child, we either have to change the place or change the child. Retention generally keeps the student in the same place in hope that she will somehow change.

The at-risk high school students in the Stay-in-School Partnership program desperately needs credits that can be applied to graduation. They know how many credits they have and how many they need. Moreover, they know how many they are likely to earn each semester. The 17-year-old ninth grader cannot graduate before he reaches his twenty-first birthday, after which he has no legal right to a free education even if he might be so inclined. Because he has not developed the necessary skills or knowledge, he probably will not be able to pass the GED. We have seen in Chapter 1 that the teacher who runs that dropout-prevention program believes his job is to give the student as many skills as possible before he does drop out.

Later in life that student could take adult education courses to prepare for the GED, but his unpleasant memories of school might well discourage such endeavors. This student's lot may have been determined when he was retained that second time. The New York City elementary schools have special programs for the large numbers of children retained and will not hold a student back more than twice. Whether this will work, only time will tell, but in a high school near City College a guidance counselor recently discovered a young woman who was doing her ninth-grade year for the fourth time.

Rasheed's comment, above, that at a certain age "it's time to get a responsibility" was not often heard in our dialogues; nonetheless, I believe, the sentiment is widespread. Most of these students have not given up on forming an occupational identity. Even if there are conflicting selves, they still search for a self-as-my-work. If school does not fit into this self, they will leave it behind, paying no heed to the exigencies of the job market.

Easing Out

To some, teachers who suggest that students take the GED, as Rasheed reports, rather than stay in school are irresponsible. Michele Fine (1986), cited in Chapter 3, doing her ethnography in Rasheed's school in 1984–1985, criticized the ease with which students were able to drop out. A student who wished to leave, she reported, need only to go to the office and request a form. The request was always speedily granted; no one tried to dissuade the student; and there was no out-counseling. The student received no advice on jobs or other possibilities. One wondered if this was by design or by simple neglect.

Dropping out of school is not always a bad decision. A friend of mine went to great pains to drop out of Boys High School in Brooklyn before the legal age. He did not have much of a student self at that time, but he has a Ph.D. today. There are many such success stories but, of course, many more failures. When I was the director of an alternative public school, a young man came to see me about the possibility of earning a diploma. He really wanted to graduate from high school, but after I outlined his possibilities he realized that he would have to be in school until he was 21 if he was to get a regular diploma. He convinced me that that plan was unacceptable, and we agreed that he would be better off not to attend.

Another young man with whom I had worked closely as a learning disabilities teacher found himself at 16 in the ninth grade, absolutely hating school. He was quite a good self-taught mechanic, had worked at various jobs, and was convinced he could find work. What he saw, if he continued school, was reading assignment after reading assignment of texts that were beyond him, low grades, boredom, and little prospect of ever graduating. He approached me about quitting and, because his decision seemed thoughtful and mature, I supported him.

There are a number of educators who believe that their major responsibility is to teach those who want to learn. Their classrooms, they think, would be better off if unwilling students left. Easing a student out of school, to them, might be the best thing possible for everybody. Whatever the reason, there is an easing-out phenomenon in our high schools where students are actually encouraged to leave by educators. Because this can never be an official policy, it is conducted sub rosa and, for good or ill, it is a reaction to intolerable situations, intolerable for both students and teachers. Simply condemning educators who engage in these easing-out procedures will not solve the problem. I do not regret counseling students to leave school.

THE IDEAL STUDENT

It would seem that those who have a fully developed student self successfully integrated with other selves are the ideal. And what is the ideal student in society's eyes? What would most parents like to see their students do in high school? What would most educators like to see students do? I would like to attempt a description of the ideal student in most people's minds.

First of all, the ideal student is in the college prep program. Even though half the population does not go on to college, many more than that start high school in the college track. School clubs and student government are dominated by college prep students. Teachers perceive that college-track classes have more able students and that perception becomes self-fulfilling prophecy. On intake interviews for our high school program, the majority of our at-risk students stated that they meant to go to college, even though few of them ever managed to graduate from high school.

In the college track, our ideal student carries five subjects a year, usually including English, math, a foreign language, a science, social studies. The ideal student gets A's and B's in these subjects; there must be room for improvement. In class, she answers questions and participates in discussions. Assignments are handed in on time; papers are neat; the appropriate books and materials are brought to class.

The ideal student participates in extracurricular activities. For boys, athletics have more prestige than clubs. Those who participate in athletics practice every day and may play a game on weekends; both teams and clubs go on trips to other schools. Those who participate in these activities get reinforcement from teachers and are often lauded to the student body. One does not have to be on the college track to participate in athletics, but most people who participate in clubs, newspapers, yearbooks, and so forth, are.

Our ideal student does his homework. If he does a half hour's homework for each major subject, not an inappropriate estimate, that is two-and-a-half hours a night. This student, therefore, takes a full load of courses, participates in an extracurricular activity every afternoon, goes home, has supper, and does his homework, which should take him close to bedtime. On weekends, there might be a sporting event to attend, if not play. In addition, there might be a social event, for example, a dance or a school play. The time of the ideal student, then, is almost totally taken up by school and school-related activities.

If this sounds idealistic rather than ideal, remember that it is this type of student who gets into our best colleges. And it is this ideal that many, if not most, of our teachers may well have aspired to when they were in school. It is also an ideal that is totally unrealistic for those who are in the wrong places at the wrong times. They do not enjoy the four-year moratorium that their college-bound peers do after high school to develop their career selves. They are more concerned with job skills than Shakespeare, employment possibilities than French verbs, meaningful work than debating.

Vocational, cooperative education, and technology programs should be considered alternative roads for other kinds of students. In many parts of the country, however, students who choose these options are derogatorily called "greasers" or other such appellations. In other areas, vocational programs come too late in a person's school career. Yet, in places like New York City, one has to choose a vocational program before she is ready or be consigned to a comprehensive high school. Such was the case for most of those in our programs. Nevertheless, variations of such programs can, I believe, change high schools to the right places.

STUDENT PERCEPTIONS OF SCHOOL

The students in our population do not see grading as an economic system, nor do they think their being eased out of school is a dereliction of duty by teachers. To them, students who achieve are nerds rather than ideals to emulate. What they criticize in school is different from what I criticize. As a group, they have rather ambivalent feelings about what should be changed and how those changes should be made to make schools better places. Along with teachers, parents, and each other, they create their own student selves, such as they are.

When asked their opinions of school, most of our students express dissatisfaction. But, just as it might be typical to complain about parents, so might it be the same about school, especially if asked by another student. Some of the criticism, however, seems to have the ring of truth even if exaggerated. As one student, Kevin, put it,

> When we were in class, right? The teachers be coming in with their newspapers and drink their coffees, and throw some mumbo jumbo on the board, you know, and they sit there drinking their coffee. If we bring a coffee and read our newspaper, after we finish doin' the work, they go to and put up a big stink. I'm like, god damn, how come, well, if they don't want us to do it, they shouldn't do it in front of our faces. They put down two cents' worth of work and sit there and drink their coffee. I guess the teachers can do it becuz they're teachers. They get paid whether we learn or not and, frankly, they don't care whether we learn or not.

But not all of them blame their teachers. Mike is nearly 17, and he is in the ninth grade. My collaborator asked him why he got left back. Mike responded:

Because, um, it's not because it's hard, you know, it wasn't hard for me to do the work and everything. I was just lazy, that's what I am. I think that it's not that I don't have the ability to do the work, I just don't do it. Um, it's a severe laziness that I just have in myself that overcomes me a few times.

From those in the dropout-prevention program, as well, we get mixed reports. Jeffrey spoke of being absent and cutting a lot when he was in mainstream classes.

I guess Mini-School teachers are, I guess, specially trained to treat each student as an individual, which should be like that all the way around. But the Mini-School teachers pay attention to you as an individual. They know that you have your own personality. You're not like everyone else. They treat you on your own level.

Byron, however, does not like the program, finding it too restrictive. John has the opposite idea.

BYRON: When you cut, you gotta take care of Feingold, you gotta take care of Wanda and everybody else in the damn office, and they really give you a hassle. I think they should slacken up a little bit.
JOHN: They could have a good program in this Mini-School if they would just tighten up a bit. Don't let the kids get away with so much stuff.

Lydia, however, has a different concern.

I think the Mini-School is an OK program. But the people there like Jane and them. They're, they care too much. Cuz now by caring too much, it gives the kids, like a whole lot of opportunities to hurt them. And when they get hurt, they catch a little snotty attitude and that messes it up for everybody . . .

Lydia is sensitive to the feelings of her teachers. She knows that they can hurt as well as students. She echoes Jeffrey, who realizes that there is one group of teachers who treat him as an individual. But Lydia is not sure that caring teachers are the best thing. They obviously care enough about Byron to keep trying to eliminate his cutting, but he rejects this as a "hassle." Kevin does not think well of teachers. Mike, whose "severe laziness" might be a symptom of depression, blames himself for his failures.

What, then, is school for? Why do they come? When one of my collaborators asked a young man this, he was told "'It's fun, coming to school and seeing people, and except the teachers, it's great." Another said, "I hang around in the hallways." The major attraction of school seems to be that there are other young people there. No other place in the lives of these young people compares to school in terms of numbers of peers. It might be the wrong place, but it is often the only place.

And the most important activity of the school day, as discussed in Chapter 3, is lunch. Lunch is the longest time in the school day when you can hang out with your friends legitimately. When our respondents were asked how to make school a better place, the most frequent suggestion was to improve the lunches. Everyone, except one young man referred to as a nerd, complained about the food.

I think students can more easily verbalize their complaints about lunch. It would be extremely difficult for them to describe how to improve their classes. Even teachers have a hard time doing that. Students know something is wrong with school but they do not know how to make it better. Tighten up, loosen up, improve the lunch is all they can come up with.

There are indications, however, that they are aware that they lack autonomy. After Byron, who thought the teachers in his program should slacken up, began to express his dissatisfaction, my collaborator asked him why he didn't complain to anyone.

BYRON: Oh yeah, about the going to the dean business and student council and all of that? That shit don't work. I remember we had a meeting with the principal, right? About why we can't have Walkmans in the lunchroom and why we can't wear our hats and all that. He kept sayin', "OK, we're gonna do something about it." Then talk to the deans and then get something to go. He can't get tack together, I mean, I'm talkin' about, like, he said, we're gonna have another meeting in two weeks. He had the meeting and then like it's, "Well, you know it's a Board of Education rule and bullshit, bullshit." It's garbage, man. They don't care whether the student likes being in school. All they care about is comin' home with their paycheck.
COLLABORATOR: So did he do something about the Walkmans?
BYRON: Yeah, he did something. You wanna know what he did? About two weeks later and put a big sign in the Dean's office,

"Any Walkmans found or seen will be confiscated." So as hats go, you gotta take 'em off or they're gonna be snatched, and you can't get 'em back until your Moms or Pops comes in. That's a real pain in the ass. Your mother's got to come all the way down here for a five-dollar hat. God damn.

Besides autonomy, students in the dropout-prevention program were also aware of their status. Even though they said positive things about their program, some felt stigmatized because of it. "Like they have Mini-School written on the program and that's stupid. Why does everybody have to know it's a Mini-Program?" one young man complained. Another said, "Like I heard people call us, the Mini-School people, retarded." One of those who thought the Mini-School was too easy concluded, "When you get your diploma and all that, you won't be able to compete with another high school."

The student selves of these young people seem far from "ideal." They would like to get diplomas, but they do not know what they want to learn. In Chapter 1, Michael spoke of taking Civil Service tests. To him, and to the students quoted in this section, a high school diploma is, at best, a credential. Michael saw it as a hurdle in getting a job. Those who spoke well of their program seemed to be saying it made school tolerable. Their student selves are coping selves rather than learning selves. This leads one to ask what happened in their prior schooling to foster such attitudes.

LIFE BEFORE HIGH SCHOOL

Although our dialogues referred mostly to the high school experiences of our respondents, we have some data on earlier school experience from which we can make some inferences. Additionally, we can draw from what other researchers have concluded. I shall also refer to my own experiences in other settings to create a picture of the elementary schooling of our at-risk students.

Industry and Work Completion

It is between the time a child enters school and adolescence that she develops what Erik Erikson (1963) calls a sense of "industry." We looked at this briefly in the Introduction and in Chapter 1. In school the child wins recognition by producing things, and she learns the basic tools of a literate society. A sense of industry, according to

Erikson (1963), means the individual adjusting herself to the "inorganic laws of the tool world" (p. 259). The desire to bring productive situations to completion overcomes the desire to play. Work completion becomes a pleasure in life.

If the child does not experience work completion, if she despairs of her tools and skills, if she loses status among her tool partners, she develops, according to Erikson, a sense of inadequacy or inferiority. This is exactly what has happened, I believe, to most of our respondents. The at-risk students in my high school class did not believe they could write well; they did not believe they could read whole books. Rather than admit to feelings of inferiority, however, they preferred to denegrate the work and tools of school.

But why didn't these people experience work completion in all those years before we met them in our dialogues? Many teachers, I would argue, do not emphasize work completion. This is not to say that they are bad teachers or that they don't care about their students. On the contrary, the teachers I am referring to are often very sensitive to their students' feelings. Such a teacher, upon seeing that a student will not finish an assigned task within a prescribed time, will assure him that he will get partial credit. This takes some pressure off the student and makes him feel a little better.

This tactic is not limited to slower students. High school math teachers are known for giving partial credit, even though the student may get a wrong answer or may not arrive at an answer at all. I passed my second semester of calculus in college, but I estimate that I completed no more than half the problems I attempted on quizzes and tests with the correct answers. Partial credit made up the balance of my barely passing grade. I was happy to pass calculus, but I realized that I could not support myself in professions where I would have to use much mathematics; you don't get partial credit if you don't solve the equation that tells you how big a beam has to be that supports the bridge you are building.

The ethic of partial credit and credit for effort permeates our school system. By rewarding students for trying hard, even if they fail to complete most tasks, we credit ourselves with being more humane, more sensitive to our students' needs, more enlightened as educators. Certainly, our students are likely to believe we are nicer people if we follow this ethic. I do not believe, however, that we are serving them well if we allow this ethic to undermine the ethic of work completion.

The major task of teachers, even more important than the development of literacy, is to find tasks appropriate for the students' abilities, enabling them to complete the tasks successfully in the time allotted. A student must come to believe that he is able to complete what he starts. Literacy is, of course, important but it is also, according to Frank Smith (1989), oversold. In itself, literacy will not solve the problems that our respondents face. Literacy is not a finished state; "it is an attitude toward the world. A literate attitude makes learning to read and write both possible and productive" (pp. 354–355).

When I was teaching special education in Maine, the school had a student named Dale. Dale was an educable mentally retarded young man who managed, with help, to graduate from high school. We taught him to read such words as men, women, ladies, gentlemen, boys, girls, stop, go, walk, wait, right, left, and numbers up to, at least, 100. There were certain other words and expressions that Dale needed to read because he wanted to obtain a driver's license, and he worked at learning them. Dale became as literate as he wanted and needed to be. On the basis of a standardized test, we might say that Dale could barely read but he had a literate attitude.

Most of Dale's day in senior high school, however, was not spent in the classroom. He became one of the school custodians and maintenance men for both money and course credit. Dale became known as a willing worker who could finish assigned tasks. From a relative he learned how to operate machinery and drive a pickup truck. We helped Dale learn what he needed to pass the learner's permit test so he could obtain a driver's license. The state allowed him to take the test orally and he passed.

Today Dale earns his living by driving a truck and has managed to buy a small house to live in. His boss knows that Dale was in a special education program in school, but he also knows that Dale had the tenacity to graduate and that he is a good worker. Dale's teachers found tasks that he could complete, and he developed a sense of confidence rather than one of inferiority. He has a sense of industry that many of our respondents who have considerably more academic ability have yet to develop.

It is possible to remain in certain school systems for years without ever finishing a task, assigned or otherwise. I know two students who claim they have never rewritten a paper. Turning in a polished product is not one of their values. Even in shop classes I have team-taught for at-risk students in New England, there were a number of young men whose attitude toward finishing a woodwork project was "close enough." Close enough might have been a half inch off the required dimension. I had to convince them that it was not close enough to get a job even as a rough carpenter.

Happy Years

Most of our respondents do not seem happy in high school. One asks if they were ever happy in their lives before high school. In the spring of 1988, I served as a consultant to develop a qualitative evaluation of the program that our respondents attended. I engaged City College students to interview the high school people. What we wanted to know was what they remembered as the best year in their educational careers since kindergarten. We wanted to know what made that year a good one so we could compare it to the year they were spending with us.

The range of years that the group identified as its best was from third through eighth grade. No one year was identified significantly more than any other. There seemed to be, however, only two important reasons why the particular year was chosen. One was a relationship with a particular teacher; this usually occurred during the elementary years. The other usually involved the coming-together of a group of friends and the new social life that ensued.

When a particular teacher was identified as the main reason why a student had a good year, the teacher was more often female but, of course, there are more female than male teachers in the elementary grades. The teacher was described in such terms as: "She cared about me as a person," "He paid attention to me," "She wanted me to learn," "She came to my house when I was sick," "He took a real interest in me." All the responses seemed to indicate that these teachers were caring and saw the particular student as an individual.

If a student identified a good year with a coming-together of a group of friends, she was sometimes talking about events in her life that had nothing to do with school. In fact, it might be that the new social group interfered with school and a student's grades might have suffered. More often than not, this good social year occurred in upper elementary or junior high school and was the marker for the time when peer culture took precedence over anything that had to do with school.

When a teacher cared about them and when they had fun with friends were the right times for our respondents. Frank Smith (1989) is doubtful that instructional programs produce much literacy, but notes that "the personal relationship between a student and a teacher might determine whether a student learns to read" (p. 355). In addition, he calls literacy a social phenomenon in which people become literate, "not from the formal instruction they receive, but from what they read and write about and who they read and write with" (p. 355).

Our respondents give us, then, some clues about what might make school work for them. We need to have each student feel that his teacher is taking a special interest in him and that his friends are having good years with him. "Learning," Smith (1989) adds, "is a simple consequence of the company you keep" (p. 355). I would add that learning and school, if it is to be successful, must also involve work completion. The right time and the right place involves the creation of valued products.

In the Beginning

When our respondents spoke of their best years, there is an implication that school was not so good before as well as after that best year. Whether it is the structure of school, the quality of instruction, the type of learning tasks or familial, socioeconomic, or cultural factors that make the larger contribution to a student's success or failure in school cannot be determined from what our respondents say. But it may be that, in many cases, elementary school students might also be in the wrong place at the wrong time. The lack of fit may simply be more discernable by the time of senior high school. Particularly, it may be more discernable to the students themselves.

Obviously, solutions to the dropout problem in high school must begin in the early grades. The sexual self may begin at puberty; the career self might manifest itself during adolescence; but the student self begins to be constructed from kindergarten on. This socially constructed self needs input from teachers, peers, and family. Yet there did not seem to be any indications from either our respondents or the Stay-in-School Partnership students interviewed that there was any foundation on which to construct student selves.

No one referred to a golden age in school. Those who spoke of a particular teacher making a particular year their best indicated that it was an atypical year in their schooling. Many, of course, identified peers rather than teachers as determiners of their best years. It may be that they never liked school. Furthermore, since the school self is socially constructed, one is led to ask whether their family members ever liked school or if their teachers even liked teaching school.

It does not seem likely that the peer self overwhelms the student self at the very beginning of the school experience. Even though, as we have seen in Chapter 4, parents want their children to succeed in school, they may project misgivings. So might their teachers, whom we will discuss in Chapter 9. If school is not working for large numbers, it must not be working for teachers, parents, or students.

Something negative happens, it would seem, very shortly after school entry to those students whom we later classify as at risk. This something cannot be identified from our data but is probably a constellation of social factors. The fact that it did not happen to Dale indicates that innate ability is not necessarily in this constellation. Dale could develop a literate attitude with only a small degree of literacy. If our respondents were in the right places, I believe they could also develop a literate attitude.

The fact that most are still in high school in spite of their lack of success means that there is something to build a student self on. If that self could be integrated with the other selves, it might even thrive. If you ask our students what prevents them from becoming better students, most would speak of boredom. I shall therefore make boredom the subject of the next chapter.

7
Boredom

MEL: I was absent a lot of times and I was cutting class because I didn't . . . I was just bored with the whole thing. It seemed like nobody was payin' attention to me.

TARA: My sister, she wanted to drop out, cuz she said it was no use going to school because, I don't even know her reason, because I never spoke to her, you know, really about that subject. But school in general, she hated school. Every time she went she just wanted to hang out and go to some classes and the teachers were always on her back but of course, they had to be on her back for that. That's what they're there for. So she saw that, that pressure building up and she had an anger building up inside her until that exploded and she said, "Well, I'm not goin' to school." And now I think she regrets it because what she does is she stays home the whole day. She leads a very boring life; she doesn't even work.

BOREDOM IN, BOREDOM OUT

What the previous chapters have shown is that, in the minds of so many of our respondents, school promises no payoff and the material to be learned has little bearing on their lives. Many respondents deal with this by absenting themselves. Others come to school and then cut classes. When walking around the school that most of our respondents were attending, I could not help being struck by the number of empty seats. The school is not underenrolled, and the official absentee rate is not overwhelmingly high. If a student comes to school she is officially present, even if she cuts most of her classes. It appears to me that one-third to one-half of the seats are always empty.

Another striking behavior I observed is that, among the students who are present, fully half of them consistently have their heads down on their desks cushioned by their arms. Even more striking is that the teachers ignore this behavior and go right on addressing the class. It would appear that the student body as a whole, whether because of absences or dozing, is not receiving very much information, let alone learning anything.

Throughout our dialogues the word most used to characterize school is "boring." It is, of course, difficult to explain why one is bored. If material is not interesting enough to be remembered, it is difficult to describe this material to anyone who asks why it is boring. The question sometimes brings an angry response, as it did from Houston.

> I just cut, I just cut cuz I don't like any of my classes. We do math. We do two plus two, five plus five, so we go to the bathroom, we close the door.

The at-risk student is often assigned to remedial classes. From a pedagogical point of view this might make sense, but Houston has been assigned to learn the same math that he had been trying to learn for the previous ten years.

What, then, are the alternatives to boredom? The angry young man described above spends time in the boys' room. One young woman admitted to cutting many of her classes, only to spend the day riding a subway train with her friends. They seem just as bored out of class as in. Is it possible, then, to create interesting and exciting classes? I thought I heard one on a tape as I listened to it before I met with my collaborators to analyze it. The lead-in was somewhat blurred, and I deliberately skipped over the teacher's handing back assignments and restating course requirements at the beginning of class. I was not sure just what class it was or which collaborator had recorded it.

The class had apparently seen the motion picture *Gandhi*. The teacher seemed excited by her material and I could distinguish two different voices in the discussion. This discussion centered around the political effectiveness of passive resistance. I became caught up in it and mentally congratulated the teacher when she made the parallel between Gandhi and Martin Luther King. I became so interested in the class that I stopped trying to do any kind of analysis and was shocked, at the end, to hear the voice of one of my collaborators saying, "Now that was the most boringest class I have."

When we compared the various "interesting" and "boring" classes, it was difficult for my collaborators to arrive at their own meaning of boredom. The class that my collaborators agreed was the most interesting was a discussion class about the problems of youth. "Boring" classes included math, an English class discussing the play *A Raisin in the Sun*, and a social studies class that was also discussing the problems of youth. The instructors of the taped classes were all White, but my collaborators, during our analytic sessions, were not able to isolate any personal qualities of the teachers that might have made a class boring or interesting. That two classes purporting to teach the same subject matter evoked opposite evaluations makes it clear that it is not the content of the classes that our population is reacting to.

Reviewing the transcripts without my collaborators, I found two teacher descriptions that we had not analyzed together. In it, one drop-out-prevention teacher, Anne, was being discussed by a collaborator and two other students. Anne was well liked, and her classes were regarded as "good," if not interesting. "She's wild, man," was a descriptive phrase that seemed to generate agreement. Another description was of a college instructor in the collaborators' one-day-a-week program at City College. "The teacher, his name is Macmoon," [an Anglicized version of a Middle Eastern name], "and I describe his private personality the way he describes his name, Macmoon; it's cool. I'd kinda just like to have him for a friend." As my collaborators and I only analyzed data that were underlined by all three, there was no follow-up on these descriptions. Obviously, there were certain personal qualities that contributed to teacher–student bonding and, presumably, good classes.

When I analyzed all the transcripts of the classes, I found that each of the "boring" classes began with the teacher collecting assignments, giving back assignments or tests, or stating requirements and future assignments. This was the material I skipped over when I first listened to the Gandhi tape. It was simply getting the "housework" out of the way and making sure that the students knew what was expected of them. This procedure is precisely the one I apply in my own college classes. But the teacher, by laying out expectations and handing out assignments, could be viewed as judgmental by the students. Class discussions might deal with interesting material, but what might have stood out to the students was that rewards (grades) were based on their performance on tests and assignments; their past experience could lead them to predict future failure.

These data suggest that the students distinguish "good" from "boring" classes on the basis of the process rather than the content of teaching. Included in the process are certain personal qualities which can only be described in the undefined terms of our respondents ("wild," "cool") and which, since the analysis focused on student rather than teacher characteristics, cannot be translated at this point and with this data into *etic* terms for educators.

My collaborators were better at finding examples of "boring" and "interesting" than at defining the terms. "Interesting" particularly puzzled them. When I asked my collaborators what they meant by "boring," one responded, "That's when everybody puts their head down on the desk." The students, therefore, were aware of the behavior I described above, even if the teachers overlook it. Teachers ignore the behavior—as a defense mechanism, I believe—or consider themselves blessed that the students are dozing rather than being disruptive.

BOREDOM AND PRESSURE

If "boring" is the word our respondents most used in their complaints about school, "pressure" was the second most used. Obviously, there must be a general agreement and peer reinforcement that school bores people and creates pressures. Boredom and pressure exist in students' minds. But, in deciding what is boring or what creates pressure, you need input from others.

The Social Construction of Reality

Boredom, I think, can be called a socially constructed phenomenon. There are social cues as to when to be bored. The concept of social construction, and the heading for this section, come from Peter Berger and Thomas Luckmann (1967). Berger and Luckmann define "reality" as those phenomena that "we recognize as having a being independent of our own volition (we cannot 'wish them away')" (p. 1). They are talking of the everyday reality and the commonsense knowledge that we share with others. All knowledge, they argue, "is developed, transmitted, and maintained in social situations" (p. 3). Their subject is how *any* knowledge comes to be socially established as reality.

Everyone, Berger and Luckmann (1967) maintain, is born into a social world where he confronts the significant others, for example, parents, who are in charge of constructing his objective reality. Teachers are later added to the group of significant others, but when the person reaches adolescence, he can replace teachers with peers. With these peers he begins to construct a subjective reality that competes with the objective reality of the significant others imposed on him as a child. We would hope that there is an integrated balance between the objective and the subjective, but this is not always the case.

But whoever one's significant others are, they act to mediate the conventional meanings that society assigns to things. The middle-class adolescent, for example, is likely to view the world from the perspective of her middle-class significant others. The at-risk student is likely to take the perspective of his peers. Such a perspective may include feelings of anger, resignation, or boredom.

The process of constructing an objective reality is what Berger and Luckmann (1967) call "primary socialization." This involves learning the knowledge one needs to become a member of society. What they call "secondary socialization" is the "acquisition of role-specific knowledge, the roles being . . . rooted in the division of labor" (p. 138). Berger and Luckmann maintain that education is the best example of this process conducted under the direction of society.

Our respondents do not seem to be acquiring much knowledge specific to their roles in the division of labor. We saw that they seemed to have no developed career selves; yet self-production, to Berger and Luckmann (1967), is a social enterprise. I suggest that when they do not develop a career self or a student self in school, our respondents, along with their peers, attempt to construct other selves and find their own roles. But the only roles some of them have is that of bored students.

The Social Construction of Boredom

Our respondents were bored with the institution of school, and with its classes, in which they find no roles. A highly significant omission from all but one of our dialogues is any mention of what goes on in these classes. Fortunately, my collaborators recorded some of their classes as the students, apparently, do not discuss class content. The one exception was when one of my collaborators asked a student about teachers he liked.

CLARK: Ms. Johnson.
COLLABORATOR: What choo like about her?
CLARK: Science, general science.
COLLABORATOR: What choo like about general science? I mean what you be learnin'? What she be teachin'?
CLARK: Right now we doing sound and light.
COLLABORATOR: Sound and light? What's there to know about sound and light? The light you can see things better; sound you can hear things better.

My collaborator is engaged in reality construction with Clark. If Clark's comments about his science classes are put down by every student he talks with, he may come to devalue those classes. Incidentally, it was this same collaborator who, in an earlier dialogue in Chapter 1, sarcastically chided a student whose hobby was sewing who then felt obliged to retreat in the face of criticism to say that sex was his hobby and that he was only kidding about sewing. Whether he will continue sewing I do not know. Neither do I know whether Clark's interest in science will continue.

Students in this population seem to get little peer support for liking classes. In some cases, liking classes is socially harmful. A college student of mine works in a Board of Education facility where literacy skills are taught to people who have dropped out of school, and where there are classes that prepare them to take the GED. One would think that in a voluntary program student motivation would be high, but many participants are there because they have been required to attend the facility by their probation officers after some trouble with the law. My student informs me that, in this situation, those who discover they have some academic ability try to disguise it from their peers for fear of being put down, ostracized, or worse.

The situation for students who have not yet dropped out may not be so drastic, but we will see in Chapter 9 how students who achieve are often regarded by their peers. We have already seen how powerful peer pressure can be for our respondents, far more powerful than teacher reinforcement. It is a short step from hiding one's academic abilities to disparaging them. In Chapter 2 we saw students wanting to hide their illiteracy and their lack of sexual experience. The paradox here is that many of our respondents feel pressure to hide their literacy just as others try to hide their illiteracy.

But is it really boredom when students put their heads down on their desks, as my collaborator suggested? What about the simple answer that they are tired? It does not seem likely that half the students are so tired during the day that they have to sleep in school. Frequent sleeping is sometimes considered a symptom of clinical depression; even though we would not want to believe that half the students are depressed, this hypothesis might warrant clinical research. Nonetheless, the state of boredom would seem to be socially constructed by both students and teachers.

In fact, boredom is part of a socially constructed reality in which school has little value. Boredom appears to be one of a succession of steps that leads to dropping out. This succession begins simply with the inability of the student and teacher to relate to each other. Let us now consider what these steps are.

Lack of student–teacher bonding.   In the last chapter we saw that the school years students identified as their best often involved having a teacher who "cared about me," who "wanted me to learn," who "took a real interest in me." But this is not to say that every teacher must form a strong bond with every student. Personal idiosyncracies and large classes make this impossible. We would hope, however, that at some point in a student's career she will form one relationship with one teacher that is personal enough for them each to share the other's perspective. There must be someone in the student's life who values her and who values education and whom the student can remember with admiration and respect. Such a teacher can compensate for the student's lack of academic success.

Lack of academic success.   Constant discouragement without any compensations can wear down the best of us. Anyone in an unpleasant environment must change that environment or, if this is impossible, leave it. If neither of these alternatives is possible, the individual alleviates his discomfort any way he can.

Peer bonding.   Bonding among peers is a positive phenomenon that takes place with or without student–teacher bonding, with or without academic success. If there is no peer bonding the student will have serious psychological problems. But if there is no student–teacher bonding, peer concerns will overshadow those of school, and friends will become the only refuge a student has if she is discouraged about school.

Peer disparagement of school.   Disparagement can be a defense mechanism. If there is social support from peers, so much the better. Even if one is not discouraged, hearing school constantly being disparaged by his friends might be enough to cause him to disparage it. This is especially true if a student has strong bonds to those who make the disparaging remarks.

Boredom.   Boredom is actually the first absenting behavior; it is a way of internally dropping out. Furthermore, boredom gives some justification for the more active absenting behaviors that follow. But when one student spends her time riding the subway after cutting classes, and another does nothing but hang around the house after dropping out, they are not escaping boredom. The friend I referred to in Chapter 6 who dropped out of Boys High and eventually got a Ph.D. left to find a more interesting life. This is not often the case for our respondents.

In one way, however, this paradox might be considered a good thing. If there is nothing less boring than school for many of our young people, we may not have to worry about competing factors. But the opposite of boredom in these cases may not be interest. Teachers beat their heads against the wall trying to make their classes more *interesting*. Yet the students in our dialogues and my collaborators tended to describe the classes they liked as "good," rather than "interesting."

Cutting classes. Even the most successful students occasionally cut classes. It is an escape from boredom and from pressure. In a large school with a cumbersome bureaucracy, a student may be able to get away with it now and again. A teacher may overlook reporting the cut, sometimes by accident, sometimes in the hope that the particular student will stop coming to class.

Absence. Absence from school is sometimes easier to get away with than cutting. A forged letter from a parent, an intercepted letter from the school, feigning sickness to a parent are all time-tested devices to stay away from school and not get in trouble. The absence, moreover, can be an excuse not to hand in assignments given while one was not in school. The number of absences is usually the most reliable predictor of who will drop out of school.

Dropping out. The step between excessive absences and dropping out of school is, at most, a piece of paper. Filling out a form takes the illegitimacy out of not attending. Actually, the paper is not even necessary in most cases in large school districts. So many students have so many absences that they often are not tracked down. One-third of the students in the one-year program in one of the Stay-in-School Partnership's schools simply disappear the following year.

Boredom, then, is not simply a lack of interest in the content of school courses. It results from certain schooling processes, such as judgmental teachers and lack of success. What makes it so pervasive is that it is constantly constructed and reconstructed in the dialogues that students have with each other. Even if they are not physically tired, dozing in class, the chief signal that a student is bored, can be described as a lack of vitality. The phenomenon, as we have said, must also sap the vitality of teachers. What we have to do, then, is make education less judgmental and find ways for students to complete valued projects. The peer self does not have to compete with the student self, for there can be peer bonding without disparagement of school. There can be student–teacher bonding as well; such bonding was achieved by Anne and Macmoon. If boredom can be socially constructed, so can vitality. A vital school is one where teachers and students work together with a belief that what they accomplish is important.

Pressure

Pressure and boredom go hand in hand. If a student, from past experience, believes that her output will be less than successful, she might well prefer to invest her energy outside of school and deal with school by being bored. To expect students who have been judged inadequate for ten, eleven, and twelve years to submit eagerly to yet another judgmental situation without a visible payoff is folly.

But Tara's sister, in the dialogue that began this chapter, apparently expended no more energy after she had dropped out of school than before. It was "that pressure building up" that caused her to leave. Yet teachers, in my experience, do not seem to believe that their nonachieving students are under any pressure at all. They complain that such students are lackadaisical and do not care anything about their classes. In fact, students often appear to be impassive in the face of failure, missed assignments, and proddings from teachers.

If students *appear* impassive, however, it does not mean that they are. Michael's nightmare of ending up as a street beggar in Chapter 1 is a lurking fear that many of his peers might share as well. Although they feel impelled to deny the link between school and success in life, they see evidence of such links in the life-styles of numbers of adults. It is unreasonable to believe that these people feel no pressure.

A student may be reminded every day, if not in every class, that he has forgotten something, that he has failed to turn in an assignment, that he failed a quiz, that he had twenty misspelled words on a paper, that he can't recognize one out of every ten words of print. Forgetting a book or a pencil cannot be remedied because students are not let out of class—perhaps for good reason—to retrieve them. Once a quiz grade is entered into a teacher's grade book, it achieves a degree of permanence. Twenty spelling errors may be too many to look up. Inability to read ten percent of the words on a page effectively kills any understanding of that page.

So whose fault is it? It does not matter; blame is unproductive in education. If a teacher is primarily a judge of student achievement (which is certainly how this population sees teachers), not much learning will occur. But will they learn anything if there is no pressure to do so? Under the present system of courses, credits, and grades, they probably won't. I will suggest some alternatives to this system in Chapter 10, but pressure currently is unavoidable and a relaxation of pressure alone will not remedy the situation.

Dozing as Resistance

How do students resist a system where school pressures people and/or bores them without promising an ultimate payoff? Disparagement of school is obviously a form of resistance; however, it is a whispered one. Teachers are, of course, aware of it, but resistance is not often voiced in the classroom. Michele Fine (1987) concluded that student voices of resistance are silenced one way or another in classrooms. Teachers and administrators, she maintains, close certain conversations, trivialize dissent, and bureaucratize resistance (as in Byron's complaints in the last chapter about not being able to have a Walkman).

The major manifestation of resistance, in behavioral terms, is dozing. Putting your head down on the desk is a visual signal. It is difficult to believe, because of the numbers who do it, that it can be attributed to depression or fatigue. The fact that my collaborator used it to define boredom to me implies that the behavior has a shared meaning for this population. It is socially constructed just as boredom is. And because it is *passive* resistance, there is often teacher compliance.

I was not present in the class labelled by my collaborator as "the boringest" where Gandhi's tactics were discussed so I do not know if any students put their heads down on the desk. It would have been highly ironic if they did: Students, in a class on passive resistance, would be practicing it because they were bored with the class. But there is a certain sadness as well; their resistance does not have an organized purpose. Few if any of the students in the Gandhi class were aware that they were practicing what their teacher was teaching. Nor was the teacher, but the resistance must take a toll on her and her colleagues. I will elaborate on this point in Chapter 9.

TEACHING A CLASS

In Chapter 5, I referred to my teaching a class in City College's Stay-in-School Partnership program. After my collaborators and I had collected most of the data that form the basis for this book, Norman Shapiro, the director of the Stay-in-School Partnership, asked me if I was interested in teaching a course in the program. I, of course, said I was too busy, but he countered by saying that there was money enough in the budget for new tape recorders and the services of a transcriber. He suggested that I teach a course that would continue my research by using the participants to collect and analyze more data. I suddenly found time, and we called the course, "Introduction to Sociology: What Is It Like to Be a Young Person in New York?"

I began the course with some confidence, believing that I would get something out of teaching it. I believed I had more data than anyone else on the population that I would teach; I thought my twenty years of teaching adolescents would hold me in good stead; I felt that my course content would interest the students as it had interested my collaborators; I had analyzed what was ineffective with some of the same students. Finally, I was inspired by Michele Fine's (1987) suggestion:

> What if the history of schooling were written by those high school critics who remained in school and those who dropped out? What if the 'dropout problem' were studied in school as a collective critique by consumers of public education? (p. 171).

During the first class, as an introduction, I played a number of dialogues my previous collaborators had collected: Marc's admission of drug abuse, which appears in Chapter 3 of this book; the conversation among two of my collaborators and two young women on why boys had to brag about having sex (Chapter 2), and Michael's nightmare (Chapter 1). Most of the members of the class appeared fascinated and moved by what they heard. I told them of my project and that I would like to continue it with them. Lastly, I distributed tape recorders; I only had six and explained that everyone would get a chance to collect dialogues.

A quarter of my students, including a few of those who had tape recorders, were absent for my second class, which took place in the first period of the day, and another quarter were late. I did not expect there to be much student–teacher bonding in a weekly class, but at least they had not experienced a lack of success with me. Many of them were in class with their friends, but I did not know, of course, if they spent any time disparaging the course. I kept remembering dialogues of people who cut their first-period class.

COLLABORATOR: Why don't you like attending your first-period
    class?
BRENDA: Well, because it's very boring. My teacher is really, like,
    off the wall. She's really, yeah, yeah, dense, very dense, very
    boring, and it's like I wake up in the morning and I just want
    some action, some, you know, learning, you know, some excit-
    ing classes and it's, like, really boring.

Could I be boring them? I asked myself. Could they be bored
even by material about their peers? If they were, was it only because it
was the first class of the day? In another dialogue a student explained
that he didn't like getting up early in the morning.

COLLABORATOR: Do you cut class instead of coming to school, or
    do you come late on purpose so you don't have to go to that
    class?
SMOKE: Maybe it's because I get up late and by the time I get here
    and about the time the bus gets here, forget it.

The latter was the type of answer my students tended to give me
if I asked them why they were late. Because I did not know them well
enough at first, and because I did not wish to set myself up as the judge
of their behavior, I did not pursue this. Instructors at the Stay-in-
School Partnership program soon learned that they had no clout. We
felt we were in no position to remove students in a dropout-prevention
program from class, even if it seemed necessary. We had no principals
or assistant principals to rely on to back up our authority; it was just the
teachers and the students.

In the course of the class I did tell them that I would wake them
up if they put their heads down, and I urged them to do the same if I
went to sleep in class. I explained that I followed that procedure with
my City College students because, as they are going to be teachers, if I
were to let them sleep in class they might let their future students sleep
in class. The net result of this was that no one put his head down on the
desk. I was unable, however, to affect the lateness or absentee rate.

At first a few students brought in some interesting and powerful
dialogues, including that of the teenage mother in Chapter 5, but they
did not collect a great deal of data. Paying students, as I have noted, is
a much more powerful reward for work than is granting them school
credit. A collaborator's role rather than a student's role is more conducive to building personal involvement in a project. I did not have to tell

my original collaborators to stay awake, and if they were late enough to miss our meetings they didn't get paid.

Nonetheless, I would hesitate to suggest that money is the answer to involving students in their education. I wonder if, in spite of the fact that some students with tape recorders absented themselves, they would have done better if each had a tape recorder at all times, as my original collaborators had. It might have made them more aware of the conversations around them and the total number of recordings might have increased. The hands-on experience would have reminded them of their roles in the project. And they would have been carrying their tools with them, an ingredient of one's identity.

I also wonder if their behavior was a reaction to school in general rather than to my class. They were always interested in listening to tapes that their peers had collected. They were less interested in my analyses and reluctant to offer their own. But they were in a school setting; they came to class at a certain time and sat at desks. They remained in their seats for another set period of time. I would take attendance and turn in my list at the end of each period. Perhaps they didn't need anyone in a school to tell them what it was like to be a young person in New York.

In some classes students were willing to talk about themselves; in others they were not. One student in the original dialogues complained about being asked to make personal revelations.

COLLABORATOR: What happened in Mr. Steppin's class?
LOUIS: You know like them questions he was giving us, you know
    I hate them personal questions, they be gettin' all personal.
    Sometimes I keep quiet.

Simply trying to make course content relevant to the lives of students is not the answer to creating "good" classes.

It is probable that few of my students would have described my class as "good." I am not sure that any of them learned a great deal, nor can I say that they looked at the world with any kind of different perspective as a result of the course. A successful educational experience for these young people, I believe, would have to last for a long-enough period of time for there to be some kind of bonding. Moreover, the students and I would have to be collaborators on a project that we all thought worthwhile. Hands-on experiences would have to replace the usual teacher-directed classroom interaction. Such experiences would lead to building skills and learning to use tools, whether those tools were hammers, typewriters, computers, or books. The rewards could be intrinsic to the activity and involve a completed project, or extrinsic like the pay my collaborators earned, or perhaps even a grade.

BORED TO TEARS: A SUMMARY

School, unfortunately, has not been able to deal successfully with pressures that students feel; indeed, it only seems to create more pressure. It has been unable to answer the most-asked question of this population, "Where do I fit in?" and much of what goes on in classes was judged as boring. One class that I judged excellent was perceived as boring by the consumers. There was evidence that what made a class boring was its process rather than its content. Personal characteristics of teachers, although they could not be specifically enumerated by the students, and teachers acting in a nonjudgmental manner were identified as factors contributing to interesting classes. There seemed to be a link between pressure and boredom, as though boredom were a passive way to drop out of school. Behaviors that stemmed from boredom were considered to be forms of resistance. Even a class that attempted to apply the lessons gathered from the collected data was not successful. Its lack of success indicates that the structure of school itself, with its defined roles for teacher and student, is a significant contributor to the dropout phenomenon.

8
Drugs

The specter of drugs was always present in our dialogues. Most of the boys—my collaborators say, all—have used some illegal substance at one time or another. They use a wide variety of substances: various distinct grades of marijuana, hashish, pills (notably, what they call Quaaludes). There was no mention of heroin; cocaine and, in particular, crack were most often mentioned. Girls in our dialogues tend to deny using drugs or alcohol, much as they deny engaging in sex. Below are examples from three dialogues in our data.

COLLABORATOR 1:   Do you go up with your friends and either do you take drugs or do your friends?
MARVIN: Well, um, some of my friends smoke. They just, like, smoking or tried crack once.

COLLABORATOR 2:   Oh man, what are some of the drugs that you sell?
DEALER: Crack, blow, smoke, everything.

COLLABORATOR 3:   What's going to happen if you can't get crack anymore? Are you serious into the drug, or do you just take it once in awhile?
JOHNNY: I've just taken it once or twice, that's all.

WHY DO YOUNG PEOPLE TAKE DRUGS?

Drug abuse is consistently the most discussed and written-about social problem in our media. Obviously it can be related to the dropout problem. Many dropouts abuse drugs; many drug abusers are dropouts. Similar messages are sent to young people about these two problems. I have mentioned celebrities who go on TV and make pronouncements, such as "Stay in school!" as if the decision to drop out was made by a individual in a vacuum. Celebrities say, similarly, about drugs, "Just say no!"

But what should they say no to? I say, they should say no to the drug scourge that is destroying large numbers of our citizens. But for them, this argument is remote. A better argument is that they should say no to something that may destroy them themselves. But this may apply as well to drinking and smoking, and there are millions of people who can't say no to these. Saying no to staying out of trouble with the law might be convincing if the substance abuse problem were not so pervasive, and the legal system so often ineffective.

On the most personal level, we are asking them to say no to something that makes them feel good. Alcohol abusers like to be drunk. Drug abusers like to be high. Society ignores the inconvenient reality that the euphoria resulting from drug use is probably the most intense and gratifying experience many people have ever had. Those who have not experienced it often display curiosity about it. How many of the readers of this book, for instance, would consider using crack, in a controlled experiment, just to see how it feels? As far as our respondents are concerned, trying something with a friend is a controlled experiment. After the experiment, if the impact of the euphoria is greater than that of the verbal arguments against drug use, they may well try it a second time.

When my collaborators asked respondents why they used drugs, they got different answers. Some reject the notion of drug abuse as an escape, seeing it only as an enhanced sensation.

COLLABORATOR: How about, do you have any, do you smoke marijuana or T-bone or something like that?

LEN: No! . . . Yeah . . . no.

COLLABORATOR: Yes and no, what is it?

LEN: Yeah, no, yeah.

COLLABORATOR: OK, do you smoke it usually when you have problems, or do you smoke it just to smoke it?

LEN: Smoke it; it's fun. All your friends get together and go to the movies, you buy the smoke and then look, like, the movie look different.

COLLABORATOR: OK, but do you take the T and marijuana for your problems, or do you just take it to have fun or whatever?

LEN: To have fun, man. Who smokes marijuana cuz they got problems? Anyway, that's stupid!

Others, however, do see it as an escape. Lee, who we met in Chapters 2 and 3, felt unloved by her parents but was buoyed up by her friends.

COLLABORATOR: Have you ever thought of leaving home or anything like that?
LEE: Well, yeah, lots of times I wanted to leave . . . just either go into something that will constantly keep me happy, like drugs . . .

Ronnie, one of the young men who had impregnated a woman, was questioned by the same collaborator on how he planned on solving his problem.

The only way out of it, from my point of view, is smoking or try to forget about it.

Peer influence seems to be the major factor in drug experimentation. One young man, Josh, complained to one of my collaborators about this.

My friends smoke crack, so then they don't tell me. I just . . . I feel it . . . I feel left out.

You won't know drugs make you feel good if no one tells you. But it is the sensations themselves from drugs that appear to be the major factors in abuse (of course, the word "abuse" is an adult word; our respondents might simply say "drug use"). To maintain that young people take drugs to escape their problems is to ascribe drug abuse to individual neurosis. It is like ascribing the problem of homelessness to individual psychosis rather than to socioeconomic causes. But drugs have enough of their own power over human physiology to become social problems.

THE CULTURE OF DRUGS

In Chapter 3, we speculated on whether the way of life of the "less literate" could be considered a culture or, at least, a socially transmitted subculture that has its own values, ways of thinking, and economic life. Whether this way of life fits any definition of culture is arguable but, if it does, that culture would have to be an adaptive rather than a maladaptive phenomenon. What our respondents and their peers seemed to be creating was a holding environment with a distinct value system, with common means of cognition and communication, and which is often the only access to the job market these people have.

If we believe there is a subculture of the less literate we can certainly believe that there is one that centers around and is driven by drugs. But such a culture is necessarily pernicious while the culture of the less literate is not; in order for the former to flourish there must be a rejection of the values of the larger culture. Can a pernicious subculture be anything but maladaptive? In the long run, perhaps not, but it may not be perceived as such by its members.

I suggested above that a drug euphoria might be the most intense and gratifying experience that some of our respondents have ever had. Winning my first medal in track may have been the high point of my high school experience but not theirs. Our respondents tend not to be involved in school activities. I enjoy films, but a bottle of crack, the drug that produces the most sensation, is cheaper than a movie. Listening to music is a great source of enjoyment for them, but it is a passive endeavor and is not precluded by drug use. Some of them might argue that drugs enhance music. For these young people, drug users have more fun.

Drugs and the Good Life

Lola Ingram (1988), a student of mine at City College doing field work in a neighboring junior high school, writes in an assigned case study:

> Most of the older boys who stay around the school are hoods. They wear gold on the necks and on their fingers, beepers on their belt waist, and drive BMW's, Jeeps, and I've seen a few Jaguars waiting outside the school. None of these boys have jobs; that is the sad part of it. Their "occupations" are scramblers, guys who sell drugs, particularly cocaine in its rock form "crack." Fast cars and young girls in the front seat grinning from ear to ear wearing hair extensions and gold jewelry everywhere.

But are these young men and grinning girls in gold numerous enough to be anything but bad examples? One of my collaborators experienced their influence close to home when he engaged a young man, still in school, in a dialogue. The young man had a car and claimed to be making $2,000 per week by supplying drugs to two other people to sell for him. On the tape that contained the following dialogue there were no names. The "dealer" apparently trusted my collaborator or had a vested interest for submitting to the interview.

COLLABORATOR: A couple of G's, that's a couple of thousand.
DEALER: Yeah.
COLLABORATOR: So how much one crack bottle cost? Like if I wanted to buy one, or three or four. How much would that cost?
DEALER: Well, I sell 'em for $10.
COLLABORATOR: Wow, that's really expensive.
DEALER: Well if you want to come into this business, you know.
COLLABORATOR: Uh, not really, not right now. I'll call you, all right?
DEALER: Yeah, you just call me and I'll be right there.

My collaborator never made the call but, although the $10 per hour I was paying him was more than twice what McDonald's would pay, it was paltry compared to what the dealer offered. Incidentally, the dialogue took place in 1987 and the $10 price the dealer quoted is now generally half that. I am told that dealers compensate for the reduced price by having more customers. The profits are still high.

Drugs and Sex

Jaguars and jeeps may give some young men access to junior high school girls, but even among those without those status symbols, it's the boys with the drugs who get the girls. In Chapter 2, we saw that two young men who claimed to have gotten women pregnant were heavy drug users. Marc, the drug addict who broke down in tears, was believed by my collaborators when he spoke, without bragging, of having sex with four different women in one week.

It may be that the young women who abuse drugs are also the young women more willing to engage in sex. And drugs do cost money; drugs in exchange for sex is common among all ages of abusers. Where young men in our data sample have a smaller pool of sexually available women than women do of men, the link between drugs and sex may be a powerful draw in favor of drug use. It may be perceived by many young men that not only do drug users have more fun, they have more sex.

As long as drugs remain one of this nation's biggest businesses, they will be available to high school students. Notions about legalizing drugs to take the profit out seem silly when the price of crack is cheaper than a movie. Obviously, plenty of profits are being made even at this cheap price. Legalization would only increase the supply of a substance that creates its own demand. An almost unlimited supply of substances that people enjoy guarantees the existence of a subculture of drugs that compounds the dropout problem.

MALADAPTATION

If there is a culture of drugs, how do young people function in it, knowing what they know about the physically debilitating effects and the potential legal difficulties? How do they deal with the long-term effects? More important, how do they deal with the possibility of doing harm to someone else? Larry, high on some substance while engaging in the dialogue that follows, is *not* a typical respondent in our dialogues. But virtually, all the respondents know a Larry or know of one.

COLLABORATOR: I'm interviewing this guy named Larry and I'm gonna talk to him about his problems and stuff. Larry, what are some of the problems that you have in school?

LARRY: First of all I've got too many problems, too many. It's too many problems to cope with and the problem is, you know, I like to take drugs and you know, do a couple of mesc, a couple ludes, you know luworks, ah, you know. See, it's that life is crazy, you know. And everybody, you know, comes down on me, and bothers me and the only way to get away from all that is by taking my drugs cuz that's, you know, they're my friends, they talk to me. And every time I go home and I pick up a lude and I'm up on it, if I wanta take it. If I don't, I put it back and I hear my name later, "Larry, Larry, come pick me up. . . ." So I just go for it and I pick up a little lude and I just pop it in my mouth, and tha's it. It'll set me straight for the whole day. And I go outside and play some handball, go to school first period, second period, third, fourth, I'm outta there, play handball right here in the handball court. It's about one of the things I like to do, you know. I don't like to come to school, period, so I just come and sign in and go back out. And there's nothin' that's gonna stop me from doin' what I'm doin' now unless other things in life change me. I don't know what I'm gonna do.

All right, and another thing, I gotta say it; I went to that Phoenix House [a drug treatment center], I went there, I was there about three times. But you know, they just talk to you, they put you in a room . . . it's like bein' in jail to tell you the

truth. But then like you know there's counselors in there and
they talk to you and they give you advice. They tell you what
to do, what's wrong with your life, what got you into this, what
is the cause of it, um, they also give you a room to stay in, but,
you know, it's like jail; it's like going. . . . I got locked up before. See, that's another story. I got locked up cuz of the problems I wuz having and I just couldn't cope with it no more. I
wuz gettin' outta hand, you know. I wanted some smoke so I
went down the block to this spot and then I told this guy, give
me some dope and he didn't want to give it to me cuz I didn't
have no money, right? So I just pulled a toolie [a pistol] and
bust some caps on [shot] him and just took it. And I got caught
for that and I got put away, cuz luckily the guy didn't die cuz I
would still be doin' time. I did three years, you know and now
I'm doin' seven years probation, which is all right for me but not
really all right cuz it's hard for me to stay out of trouble, and if I
get caught again, I'll be doin', God knows, twenty to life if I get
outta hand again. So I'm gonna try Phoenix one last time . . .

Larry's existence should be an object lesson to anyone who uses or
is considering using drugs. Listening to him should be a greater deter-
rent to taking drugs than drug education. Apparently, however, every
drug user is convinced that he will not become a Larry.

COLLABORATOR: Are you ever afraid of getting addicted to crack?
ROLAND: Well, people say once you take it you get addicted to it.
COLLABORATOR: Well, don't you think you're addicted to it?
ROLAND: No, I could stop anytime. I just wanna do it for pleasure.

Another collaborator asked a user, Lyman, how he would stop using
drugs if he had to.

If you're in a situation where it's too much, just break out.

Besides not fearing addiction, some of our respondents did not
seem to fear physically damaging themselves, nor even risking death.
Francisco, whom we met in Chapter 3, if he is to be believed, is one of
these. Near the end of his dialogue about drugs and friends, my
collaborator was stymied on how to deal with him.

COLLABORATOR: So, what's . . . ? What's . . . do you try to stop
   or . . .
FRANCISCO: You only live once, so live it up!

COLLABORATOR: OK, if that's the way you think, I respect your
    way of thinking.
FRANCISCO: If I die, I die . . . if I don't, I don't.
COLLABORATOR: OK, um . . .
FRANCISCO: Either way you're gonna die sooner or later.

Nor do some of them fear legal retribution. In Chapter 2, we met
Syl, a drug user who had contempt for women.

COLLABORATOR: You're only 16. Don't you . . . have you ever
    thought of being something in life.
SYL: Crack dealer.
COLLABORATOR: OK, you think that's a good future? I mean do
    you think that's something positive, like when you go out in the
    streets and sell crack, do you think that you're always going to
    be doing that or you're going to be caught one day and be in
    jail for life.
SYL: Well I doubt you could be in jail for life for crack.
COLLABORATOR: Yeah, well, yeah. I was just saying that, you
    know, to see . . .
SYL: But if I'm in jail, that's my other home, so that's the whole
    point, as long as I'm livin'.

We may doubt the almost boastful remarks of Francisco and Syl,
and it may be that when they are in those marginal situations, when
they actually face jail or death, they may express other attitudes. We
would like to think that Larry, Francisco, Roland, and Syl are the
exceptions in our high school population. But their numbers seem to be
increasing and, as a result, the attitudes they express are magnified.
Worse, it does not seem that they can be reached through most educational situations.

A DIFFERENT BALL GAME

When my collaborators and I analyzed the first round of data collected
in the spring of 1987, I did not envision drugs as a major facet of the
dropout problem. In an article based on that part of the data that
appeared in 1988 I wrote that "there was no evidence in the data that
substance addiction was typical among the people interviewed." I had
experienced students using drugs and had counseled them for years,
but I believed most such use to be experimentation only. Some of my
colleagues disagreed with me when I maintained that anyone caught

selling drugs in school should be prosecuted. Even though I still advocate this, my position implies that the problem is solvable and that its impact can be removed from schools.

When I originally planned this book, I did not intend to have a separate chapter on drugs. I did not wish to minimize the problem, but my concern was with high school being the wrong place at the wrong time; if we could just improve the educational system, we could lower the dropout rate. Improved education could then contribute to the solution of other social problems. I have been a schoolteacher for most of my life. To people like me, education is the answer to many social problems.

Obviously, I was not unaware of the social context of education. That was what this research was all about. The question that I instructed my collaborators to center their dialogues on had to do with what it was like to be a young person in the particular area in which they lived. Only by understanding this could we hope to develop any kind of dropout-prevention program. But as great as I realized the drug problem was, I considered it only a part of the social context I was investigating. After all, only a small minority of people ever became addicts.

Moreover, those few who were addicts were beyond education. If a young person were still in school, I reasoned, no matter how tenuous her hold on education might be, she still must have some kind of belief that she can benefit from it. Additionally, because of my faith in the process, I thought school was the only place where we could institute drug education programs. School was no place for addicts but the only place for prevention.

However, the latest information (see Moynihan, 1989), along with what I hear on the streets and from my students and former collaborators, leads me to believe that my previous beliefs and the results of my original analysis of the first round of data are now outdated. Increased drug use, especially of crack, creates a whole new ball game for young people, not only in the cities but everywhere.

The crack epidemic is most noticeable in urban areas but expands daily. In New York City, the site where our data was gathered, there are 1.1 million inhabitants between the ages of 15 and 24. No one knows, of course, how many crack users there are, but Senator Daniel Patrick Moynihan (1989), a member of the Senate working group on substance abuse, cites what he calls "responsible estimates" as high as 600,000. Doubtless, the latter figure include users older than 24, but the numbers are nevertheless astounding. The word "epidemic" may often be overused, but with these numbers it is totally justifiable. Crack has only been in evidence in New York since 1985.

Crack is made from cocaine. It is crystallized by processing it with other chemicals. Cocaine is expensive, but billions of dollars' worth of it come into this country. The United States is the largest importer of cocaine in the world. It is obvious that importing an expensive drug and processing it must entail capital, organization, and effort. Cocaine, a powder that is inhaled or sometimes injected, is bought principally by more affluent users.

But crack is cheap. A little cocaine goes a long way in the processing. As of this writing, crack usually sells on the street for $5 a bottle. I have even heard of it selling for as little as $3. A bottle is a small sealed glass with a few crystals of the drug in it; the crystals are placed in a pipe and smoked. It is easy to conceal and is one of the most portable of drugs. One cannot very easily bring a six-pack of beer or a bottle of whiskey into school, but crack is another story.

Crack is a stimulant. It is easier to use than an intravenous drug. The effects it produces, as we have said, are more intense than perhaps those of any other drug. This intensity is immediate but short-lived. Therefore, repeating the euphoria demands more frequent use of crack than of most other drugs. For these reasons, it is considered one of the most addictive substances available. It has been rumored that some people have become addicted after using as few as six bottles. Such rumors are impossible to document, and we do not wish to attempt to establish the ease of addiction by experiment in a laboratory. In July 1989, it was reported that a new drug combination of smokable heroin and crack was being sold on the streets; the mixture prolongs the euphoria but is even more addictive.

But just what *addiction* means is not clear. None of our respondents who used crack would admit to being addicted. Using the most addictive drug available is obviously a self-destructive behavior. Unfortunately, it is physically as well as mentally destructive. Senator Moynihan's (1989) committee has heard testimony that the time from first use to debilitation can be as little as six weeks. It does not seem that crack use can ever be called "experimentation"; indeed, it might be the most serious social problem we have.

The crack problem could prove to be of such immense proportions as to dwarf the dropout problem by comparison. If crack is not controlled, it could destroy the generation of youth that we are concerned with here. And this problem does not have an imminent solution. The development of a pharmacological block that would be to cocaine as methadone is to heroin is a bad solution but, many authorities agree, might be the only solution. Education that is offered in the wrong place at the wrong time, that cannot convince these young people of the benefits of schooling will probably not be able to convince them of the dangers of drug abuse. At any rate, it has not yet.

SELF AS USER

In the context of the theory that organizes this book, what crack or another drug might do is offer the basis for another self, one that I did not count on when I planned the book. This is a self-as-(substance)-user. This may seem bizarre but the user self can actually become the primary self of the adolescent and the one within which a number of the other selves can be integrated: sexual self, peer self, and even career self.

I have suggested elsewhere that the sexual self can overwhelm all other selves. But we have also seen that sex is peripheral to the lives of heavy drug users, even though they might engage in sexual behavior more often than their peers. Sex is the principal change that separates the period of adolescence from all that has gone before. But drug abuse might actually become the principal change factor as far as young people's behavior is concerned. Teachers and parents have often been shocked at the difference in personality in adolescents after the adolescents begin to abuse drugs.

Access to drugs can give a young person status among his peers, at least among a certain number of them. As Francisco admitted, substance abuse may not make for lasting friendships, but there are always people to do drugs with. Those people, of course, give a kind of support to drug abuse. To deal drugs you must automatically step into a social network. This network no longer consists of furtive groups of people always looking over their shoulders. It is a group characterized by fancy cars and gold chains.

To call drug dealing a career can be either a joke or an insult, but the "work" of the dealer is selling his wares. It is a "tangible adult task," to quote Erik Erikson (1963), which has its own role models and "occupational prototypes." Most important, it offers the highest degree of financial success. The author James Baldwin has said that when he was growing up in Harlem, there were only two roads to success: religion and crime. Many at-risk students see drug dealing as the only road to success.

To the addict, it would seem, substance use *is* his identity. There are no other concerns. An addict consolidates all his anxieties and cares into one, just as some people take out loans to consolidate all their debts. The only worry that the addict has is where his next fix or hit is coming from. If there is a financial source to pay for this, like dealing or a boyfriend who is dealing, the euphoria pushes the anxieties away. Even reformed addicts often hold onto their addicted selves.

Drug use makes for a perverted socialization, but a socialization nonetheless. Berger and Luckmann (1967), whose ideas on the construction of objective reality were the basis of our discussion of boredom in the last chapter, also discuss "subjective reality," which concerns the process of socialization in a personal way: how an individual becomes a part of his society. They distinguish between two types of socialization: primary and secondary.

Primary socialization has to do with the individual learning from significant others about the social world and the values he is born into. This process is complete when the "generalized other" is established within the individual. The generalized other is George Herbert Mead's (1934) term for the voice of society; it is the internal Greek chorus we answer to for our decisions and our behavior. But each individual has a more or less distinct generalized other. A lower-class child has a lower-class perspective colored by that of her parents. In this she may be content, resigned, or resentful. The social world she inhabits is different from that of an upper-class child.

Secondary socialization entails the learning of role-specific knowledge, the roles, according to Berger and Luckmann (1967), being rooted in the division of labor. In this, they are not far from Erikson's (1963) concept of identity. The most satisfactory socialization occurs when there is a balance between the primary and the secondary components. The individual must have a knowledge of the social world and know where he fits into its division of labor. Socialization is rounded out when all selves are integrated.

Primary and secondary socialization, however, are not always in balance. The young person who graduates from college with a major in fine arts may have attained a fairly complete knowledge of the social structure and its accompanying values, and therefore attained a high degree of primary socialization. But if he cannot find a job he may not have attained a very high degree of secondary socialization. His socialization might not be very satisfactory either to himself or his parents who are paying his bills.

The drug dealer, on the other hand, may not have very much knowledge or concern for the social structure and its values, but might have a great deal of role-specific knowledge. He may have an uncanny understanding of the culture of drugs and may know exactly how he fits in. Not only that, but it may be an excellent fit. Such a person would have a high degree of secondary socialization, but would not have developed much primary socialization. I would call this kind of socialization perverted.

The user self has integrated a number of selves, but is prohibited from integrating all of them. He will never become educated, be a normal parent, and probably not have a genuine love relationship. Ultimately, the user may go to jail, become a hopeless addict, be killed by drugs, or be murdered. In the meantime, however, he may sell his wares to others and, with his Porsche and grinning girls, become the wrong kind of role model for another generation.

WHAT CAN WE DO IN SCHOOL?

Is there anything we can do in our schools to combat the problem? If we believe no, we must either leave the teaching profession or prowl the halls of our schools with baseball bats. If I thought baseball bats were the only answer, I would issue them to teachers. But we would lose our selves in the process.

Obviously, we must try to confront the problem, but first we must determine who "we" are. To have teachers giving out information about drug use to students who know more about it than they do is, obviously, not an effective program. Any drug program must have the input of both students and teachers. Moreover, the students should not be those chosen by teachers: school "leaders," those with high grades, etc. The at-risk students offer a better pool.

Additionally, informal rather than formal programs might work better. My collaborator, though untrained, functioned superbly as a therapist in his dialogue with Marc in Chapter 3. He tells Marc to "hang on my shoulder," but does *not* tell him to stop using. Instead of offering alternative life-styles to a life of abuse, he asks Marc what he would like to be doing if he were not using. He offers support with, "You could stop when you feel you're ready to," and "Any time you want to talk to me, you could just talk to me." Finally, he is impassionate rather than dispassionate when Marc breaks down, and effects a kind of catharsis in Marc. If a psychotherapist had a similar "therapy hour" with Marc, he would feel professionally rewarded and closer to a positive prognosis.

We must use the selves that are already developed in these young people to integrate the other selves. The self-as-loyal-friend is not only the best vehicle to use, it is the only real vehicle with any chance of success. We cannot expect to lure a young person from a user self, which may also include a sexual self, with only the prospect of a student self. True, the young mother in Chapter 5 left a user self behind for a parent self. We cannot, however, suggest pregnancy as a alternative to drugs.

A self-as-loyal-friend within the context of building a career self may offer the best kind of therapy, especially when there are few therapists in proportion to the number of drug users. A group of friends with a common purpose makes for the best kind of holding environment, to again use Winnicott's (1971) term. If there is an adult involved, she becomes a representative of and a conduit to the larger culture. This adult can be a youth worker, a boss, or a teacher.

Because all children go to school, teachers would be logical candidates for this role. But could such holding environments be created in the schools? Roles in schools are often rigidly prescribed. Can we enlist students and teachers into small groups that can develop this holding capacity? In the last chapter I will describe such an environment. If that environment cannot be created within the schools, I believe it can, at least, be created within a school system.

The exploding drug problem makes it imperative that something be done now to alleviate the problems of young people. The at-risk student is more susceptible to the lure of drugs than his more successful peers. Middle-class and college-bound students can be victims as well, but they have support systems that the at-risk student lacks. Nevertheless, if any students in a school are substance abusers, drugs are that much closer to everyone. As the dropout and the substance abuse problem interact, they cannot be addressed separately. Obviously, then, they must both be addressed by our educational system. In the words of H. G. Wells, we have a "race between education and catastrophe."

9
Conflicting Meanings of School

This book has been organized around a theory of "conflicting selves," which attempts to explain how the inability to integrate these selves acts to prevent the individual from being adequately educated and integrated into the larger society. Although these selves were always in relation to others, the theory is a social *psychological* one that does not explain how at-risk students as a group differ in their thinking from other groups they come into contact with, notably their teachers and those students who *are* able to integrate their selves. School must have a different meaning to these groups, and such meaning must be socially constructed. An understanding of this is essential to educators of at-risk students.

We have already speculated on whether there was a subculture of the less literate that was in conflict with the larger culture that surrounds it. I suggested that there was such a subculture that acted as an adaptive mechanism to create a holding environment within the larger and perhaps threatening culture. How such a subculture is created, however, was not made clear. What is needed is analysis that clarifies the nebulous notion of culture.

We saw in Chapter 1 how Wilson (1987) analyzed the effects of economic forces on the lives of working-class people. Economic forces, however, only act indirectly on education. To be sure, those forces affected their families, but few of our respondents seemed to have a clear idea of the meaning of economics to their lives and their education. Neither did they seem to attach a meaning to anything we can call social class. Again, analysis is needed that explores the way at-risk students find meaning in their lives.

134

MEANING SYSTEMS

Frederick Erickson (1986) has advocated that we explore the "conditions of meaning" or "meaning systems" that enable some students to learn and others not. Erickson (1976) engaged in microanalyses of interactions to investigate meaning systems and, as an ethnographer, looked for his theory to arise from his data. Returning to analysis on a more global level, Berger and Luckmann (1967) have introduced the concept of "legitimation" as a social process by which individuals objectify meaning. The highest level of legitimation, they tell us, involves the creation of "symbolic universes."

Symbolic universes are all-encompassing meaning systems; they are social products with a history. A symbolic universe integrates all institutional processes and enables the individual to make sense of the entire society. It supplies order for the different phases of one's biography. Individual realities can be encompassed into this overarching universe of meaning. Symbolic universes are handed down from one generation to another, but some individuals, Berger and Luckmann (1967) maintain, "inhabit" the transmitted universe more definitely than others. The college-bound high school student, for instance, "inhabits" the overarching system that gives meaning to school more definitely than does the at-risk student.

Moreover, modern societies are pluralistic. Berger and Luckmann's (1967) symbolic universe is a core universe that coexists with any number of partial universes. However, they point out, a pluralistic society *presupposes* an urban society with a complex division of labor, a high differentiation in the social structure, and a *high economic surplus*. Wilson (1987), however, presents evidence that for the population that yielded the data for this book and for any population where the working class faces a loss of job opportunities, economic surpluses are not always available. Those who are left out may also have only a tenuous hold on the overarching universe.

Does such an abstract concept really have an effect on marginal high school students? The lack of an overarching system of meaning, I would argue, affects this population more than others. Berger and Luckmann (1967) believe that a major function of such a system is to enable the individual to make sense of what they call "marginal situations." Anticipation of death is *the* marginal situation, but on the general level of meaning, institutional order (read, symbolic universe) represents a shield against terror. Michael's nightmare of becoming a street beggar (Chapter 1) is an example of such terror. He cannot make sense of the fact that there are street beggars in the American society he has read about in his textbooks or been told about by his teachers.

An intrinsic problem with handing down a symbolic universe to the next generation, according to Berger and Luckmann (1967), is the possibility of deviant versions of such a universe coming to be shared by groups of inhabitants. When a symbolic universe has become a problem, as it has with Michael and the less literate in general, what Berger and Luckmann call "universe maintenance" becomes necessary. In this context, conceptual machineries of universe maintenance include mythology, theology, therapy, and nihilation.

Mythology.   Myth acts on the least sophisticated level of universe maintenance. George Washington's never telling a lie and Abe Lincoln's walking miles in the snow to return a few cents he had inadvertently shortchanged a customer were myths I was taught in school to impress upon me that honesty is the best policy. Horatio Alger gave a generation or more of Americans a positive mythology of our economic system in a time when great problems were arising from the conflict between unrestricted business interests and the incipient labor movement.

Theology.   Religious codification does not replace but supplements mythology in maintaining symbolic universes. The "work ethic" that we wish all our students would adopt is also the "Protestant ethic." Material success was seen by Puritans as evidence of God rewarding the good. The Protestant ethic aspired to make both rich and poor people accept the seventeenth-century reality where there was such a great discrepancy in the distribution of wealth.

Therapy.   When an individual has trouble accepting or maintaining a symbolic universe, he is a candidate for therapy. Most therapies seek to change the individual's outlook so that he will be able to adjust to society. More important for the society, therapy implies that there is a theory of deviance. Relegating such behaviors as drug use, dropping out of school, and teenage pregnancy to various pathologies enables us to see these as individual maladjustments, rather than social problems.

Nihilation.   One way to eliminate an encroachment on one's symbolic universe is by conceptually annihilating it. In my symbolic universe, education offers anyone access to the American dream. If this notion is threatened because so many young people drop out of school, I can annihilate the problem. For example, the percentage of students leaving school has actually decreased over the last hundred years; ergo, there is no dropout problem.

But nihilation is a double-edged sword. Those who do drop out and feel the effects, such as not being able to find work, must practice their own kind of nihilation: society is corrupt, unjust, hypocritical. This nihilation can lead to dangerous antisocial behavior. Articulate criminals and drug addicts have published best-selling books with this theme in order to protest their annihilation by society and to, in turn, annihilate that society as a valued institution.

WHAT SCHOOL MEANS TO EDUCATORS

The symbolic universe that is handed down to the at-risk student in school is the universe of her teachers. It is education, after all, that has given these people's lives meaning. Although they might chuckle at Horatio Alger stories, they have a mythology of sorts that supports the rags-to-riches theme, provided that they do not take the word "riches" literally.

An older math teacher at one of the first schools I taught in told the story of how as a child he was walking with his mother, and she gave a warm hello to a man they passed in the street. Afterwards she turned to her son and exclaimed, *"That* was a teacher!" A few years later I remember complaining to my analyst that all I was, was a teacher. With a look of true puzzlement, he said, "But it's a noble profession."

As an eighth grader in a Brooklyn public school, I recall my family doctor's son verbally accosting (justifiably, I thought) our absolutely terrible shop teacher outside of the school. A crowd of us soon assembled. His father happened to observe the encounter, walked over and, with considerable force, slapped his son across the face, causing both considerable pain and humiliation. He then roared, so that everyone could hear, "You *never* talk that way to a teacher!"

Years later, my doctor confided in me that he later spoke to the shop teacher privately, rebuffed the man's expressions of gratitude, and told him that he believed he *was* the worst teacher he had ever heard of. What my friend, my analyst, and my doctor had in common was that they grew up, sons of immigrant parents, on the Lower East Side of New York. The symbolic universe that was handed down to them by their parents included a mythology that bordered on theology: education was the way up; teachers were among the most respected members of society.

There are still many teachers today with the same mythology. I see a new generation of them in my graduate classes at City College, many of whom are immigrants from the Caribbean, Latin America, Africa, and Europe. Others come from the same tradition as my friend, my analyst, and my doctor. But many of an older generation who are still teaching have become frustrated, bored, angry, and burned-out. Virtually all of them, however, once had such a mythology. Part of their frustration is that far fewer members of the public share the mythology, and they have not been able to pass it on.

Teachers of at-risk students have been unable to pass on to their students the notion that education is the passport to a respectable middle-class life. Any mythology or theological beliefs they may have remain in their generation. Attempts at therapy are frustrated because the numbers of students preclude any extensive therapy and even all but the most cursory counseling. Teachers' frustration can turn to disparagement of their students, but many do not realize that their students feel an equal sense of frustration as they begin to realize that schooling, the only education they know, is not the answer for them.

Disparagement of students is a form of nihilation. The statement "They don't have enough innate intelligence; there's nothing I can do" is an example. These are not the students some teachers bargained for when they decided to take up their profession. If the students can be pushed out of one's symbolic universe or relegated to case studies, they need not be counted as one's failures. But if the symbolic universe is to encompass all reality, the teacher cannot, in good faith, push students out of it. She can, in good faith, admit that she is unable to reach all students if she will try to envision alternatives to the kind of education she practices.

As it is, alternatives are experimental and few and far between. We tend to cling to our old structures and hope that various kinds of therapy will suffice to improve schooling. What teachers tend to believe is that reaching the student on a one-to-one basis will alleviate the problems and, in Berger and Luckmann's (1967) terms, pass down and maintain their symbolic universe. I argue, however, that the meaning systems of teachers and the less literate are so divergent that therapy is not enough.

The major form of therapy practiced in schools is counseling. We have professionals hired for that purpose. To be sure, the typical guidance counselor's load makes it almost impossible for her to do anything but help students choose courses to register for. Better financed school systems would enable this type of personnel to counsel students about life problems. But, even if they have the time, guidance counselors will have a hard time reaching many of these students if their respective meaning systems have little overlap. Our dialogues have yielded an example of this lack of overlap.

THE SCROLL ON THE WALL

One of my collaborators chose to interview a staff member in his high school. He found out that her actual title was "Family Associate," a position that would seem to include both the functions of a guidance counselor and truant officer. His dialogue with her cannot, therefore, be considered a typical counselor–student interview.

The student and the counselor, Stella, were on a first-name basis and the interview proceeded with Stella, a seven-year veteran in the school system, giving her background. My subjective impression was that the conversation was warm and friendly, with Stella doing most of the talking. Stella has a Jewish background and my collaborator is nominally a Muslim, but when he asked her about her religion they found they had something in common, and the interview became a dialogue.

Stella is a member of a Buddhist sect known for chanting as a form of religious expression, prayer, or meditation. It is a proselytizing sect. My collaborator found this out when he asked her if she had any religion, and Stella found out something about my collaborator as well.

STELLA: Yes, I have a religion. I'm a Buddhist and I chant.
COLLABORATOR: I used to do that.
STELLA: Oh, you do?
COLLABORATOR: Yeah, I got the scroll and . . .
STELLA: You have one?
COLLABORATOR: No, I just got the scroll.
STELLA: Where did you get the scroll?
[Stella's speech became very animated; when my collaborator began to tell her when and where he got the scroll, she finished his story for him.]
STELLA: Okay, it was at Union Square and you got it from a priest, who put it in your hand and said you should protect this with your life? And he said it's easier to get than, . . . it's difficult to practice. So that you've heard of . . .
COLLABORATOR: I don't know.
[My collaborator finished his own story about meeting a Japanese priest and reading the group's literature. He expressed

some reservation, however, and expressed displeasure that some members of the group came to his home unannounced.]

STELLA: Well, didn't anybody even ask you about enshrining?

COLLABORATOR: He wanted too much money for that. It was a little cardboard cabinet.

STELLA: It's four dollars.

COLLABORATOR: It's a lot of money, four dollars.

[Stella volunteered that she had a wooden cabinet for her scroll that cost twenty dollars, but that she also had an extra one that she would give to my collaborator. He politely refused and complained again about some of the group members' pushiness. Stella ignored that and asked if he had returned the scroll.]

COLLABORATOR: I still have it. I put it up on my wall.

STELLA: You put it up on the wall? . . . Do you know what it is?

[When my collaborator allowed that he did not, Stella was surprised.]

STELLA: But you hung it up on your wall, and you don't even know what it is?

COLLABORATOR: They gave it to me and I paid them ten dollars.

[He explained that he did it because he likes new things. He had chanted but the chanting, apparently, had little meaning to him. Stella then interrogated him as to what he wanted in life. My collaborator said he wanted to achieve, to be part of the jet set.]

STELLA: Rasheed wants to be part of the jet set, but he doesn't even realize what he has at home.

COLLABORATOR: I just got this. It's brown with white things in the middle, with a lot of scribbling on it.

STELLA: You know what? You have it on the wall; it shouldn't just be nailed up on the wall like that.

COLLABORATOR: No, it's not nailed up.

STELLA: No, I mean it shouldn't be open on your wall, unprotected. See, what that represents is your life. You protect it like you protect your life . . .

That all three of my collaborators thought this dialogue was significant, even though on first glance it did not seem to directly address our research themes, caused me to consider it further. It seemed to be somehow linked to our conclusions that social and school pressures were persistent factors in the lives of our respondents. If Stella is correct, they were talking about my collaborator's life. It seemed that my collaborator was resisting a pressure that other people were putting on him. There is obviously no overlap in the mental representations that each of the actors establishes about the same object. He does not recognize the "life" she creates for him. Later in the dialogue, Stella explained the scroll and the sect's beliefs and informed my collaborator that the scroll does not really belong to him.

COLLABORATOR: I gotta give it back?
STELLA: Well, if you're not gonna practice it.
COLLABORATOR: I paid fifteen dollars.

From the data it appears that Stella and my collaborator have different mental representations of money. His comments indicate a scarcity of money in his life, while Stella, though probably not affluent, is comfortable. Our data suggest that money also may be less important to her than her religion. My collaborator's economic reality, then, differs from Stella's. In addition, Stella's version of my collaborator's misunderstanding of the scroll, especially after she gives it a metaphorical significance, indicates that their realities have little overlap.

The reality that Stella deals with when she interacts with my collaborator is a hypothetical one. But she is a school counselor; if she were functioning in that capacity with him, what kind of counsel could she give him? For his part, my collaborator did not learn of Stella's actual title until the beginning of the dialogue; she was not *his* counselor. When she tells him how to live his life, according to her meaning system in which his scroll *is* his life, he resists.

My collaborator, after his dialogue with Stella, remained unconvinced. He was unconvinced that the chanters were the social group for him. He was unconvinced that the scroll represented his life. He was unconvinced that the hypothetical space Stella had established for him actually had room for him. Finally, he was unconvinced that Stella's more affluent value system, in which a piece of paper was more important than his $10 (later, $15), should be his value system. One wonders how often students leave counselors unconvinced of what they were told.

What is interesting about my collaborator's lack of desire or inability to inhabit Stella's symbolic universe is that it is a universe free of many of the conflicts our respondents become involved in while trying to integrate their selves. She is *not* trying to convince him to study harder or to accept a mythology in which education is the key to success. The content of their dispute is over how much of a meaning system relatively new to both of them they are willing to share. Might this not indicate, however, that the counselor–counselee role relationship where the counselor gives most of the direction, as Stella does, is inappropriate for universe maintenance? The usual therapy applied in the schools simply may not work. I will introduce alternative therapies in the next chapter.

WHAT SCHOOL MEANS TO THE AT-RISK STUDENT

Our respondents obviously have a great deal of difficulty attributing meaning to their schooling. In the shared symbolic universe of those at-risk students who are still hanging in, still on the rolls, still trying to graduate, there must be jobs out there for them. They must make themselves believe that the good life is attainable for them through legitimate means. They must make themselves believe that, in spite of their history of failure, they will be able to complete enough courses to graduate.

Sustaining such a belief system may be an impossible task for most at-risk students. Their marginal reality is not encompassed by the symbolic universe that is handed down to them by their teachers. They seem to have no positive mythology to help them sustain their belief systems. Occasionally, they can create myths like that of the respondent in Chapter 1, who claimed that a two-week course in construction would get him a job in the trade, but not a mythology like the Horatio Alger theme of anyone who gets a job and works hard will rise to at least a decent standard of living.

We have determined that our population has no religious orientation to speak of and no theology to sustain the universe that is being handed down to them. Conventional therapies do not seem to work or, perhaps, are simply not cost-effective enough to be used with such large numbers of individuals. To maintain the universes they have, they use nihilation in the form of socially constructed disparagement of school, of teachers, and even of those who inhabit their teachers' meaning systems more definitely than they do—the "good" students.

WHAT SCHOOL MEANS TO THE "GOOD" STUDENT

Who are these students who inhabit the overarching universe more definitely than do our respondents? We have met some who were attending an "elite" high school on the City College campus. We said they had tools and skills, definite career goals, knowledge of the job market, and a belief that education gave access to that job market. Most important, although they came from the same socioeconomic groups as our at-risk students, they had a peer-support system in their school that constantly validated their beliefs in education.

Being at the A. Philip Randolph High School helped these students, but what of the students in the ordinary comprehensive school? "Good" students in a school like those of our respondents have the same socioeconomic status and may have every positive advantage the "elite" students have, except for one. They do not have the peer-support system in their school that validates and maintains their symbolic universes. On the contrary, they may have to contend with deviant universes.

We have seen how "good" students were called nerds by my collaborators. Even though they were the butts of jokes, one was able to anger his antagonist by suggesting that my collaborator had no direction in his life. The meaning systems of these students were as different from those of the at-risk students as my collaborator's was from Stella's.

SNAPPING WITH THE NERDS

When questioning my collaborators as to what a nerd was, I was not able to get a satisfactory definition. How a student dressed seemed to be one of the major criteria. One of my collaborators, in describing a particular nerd, said that he was kind of strange, "He be walkin' around with his eyes all wide open and stuff." I could not understand his comment, but I remembered that few of these students seem willing to make eye contact with me when I walk around their schools. Are nerds, then, those who have not lost their ingenuousness?

Our data contained several dialogues with nerds; my collaborators were paid by the interview, as I said, and the nerds were considered fair game. "Snapping" means trading insults. One of my collaborators, aged 17, interviewed Richard and Donald, freshmen in his school. When listening to the dialogue, one picks up a note of disdain or superiority in my collaborator's voice.

COLLABORATOR: We're here to discuss nerds, you know, the nerds in our school and nerds in general. Now, Richard, c'mon over for a second, how do you feel about drugs?

RICHARD: Well, in the first place, nerds are everyday common people. I don't know why you call us nerds. Just because we're smart, doesn't mean we're nerds, you know.

COLLABORATOR: Yeah, so?

RICHARD: So why call us nerds? What makes a nerd?

COLLABORATOR: You're pencilheads.

DONALD: I have to disagree with the term "nerds." I really feel that's inappropriate. What if we called you academically deprived? What if we call you stupid? What if we called you duds? How would you feel about that? I mean I don't really . . . it's stupid. We don't appreciate being called nerds.

COLLABORATOR: Y'all brought the word upon yourselves. Look how you dress. A plaid shirt with a checkered tie!

DONALD: And look at you! You wear beat-up, big gold chains. Now if that isn't totally grotesque. I mean, really.

COLLABORATOR: How many people have you seen in the school with pocket protectors? OK, now lookit, Richard, here. He got 40 different color pens in here.

RICHARD: You're exaggerating.

COLLABORATOR: Well, OK, OK, OK.

RICHARD: OK, OK, I bet you guys go on interviews with those same old big gold chains on. Stupid sneakers and blue jeans, and you expect to get somewhere in life dressed like that. At least we have the sense to dress the way we should dress. [The dialogue continued in this vein with the nerds protesting about being stereotyped. My collaborator is taller besides being older and perhaps somewhat intimidating, but the freshmen snap back. It is not clear who is getting the better of the argument. In my opinion, the nerds appear more agitated than my collaborator until the part, reproduced below, that we considered earlier.]

RICHARD: Can I speak, please? . . . Thank you. Thank you. What it boils down to is that you people see us as being inferior, just because we happen to have a little more common sense than you. Now we go to class. We don't cut. Now, like, why don't you all like us? I mean everyone's against us.

DONALD: I bet you don't even know what college you're going to. I bet you haven't even considered what you're gonna do after high school.

COLLABORATOR: I'm gonna go where life takes me, okay?

Is there some significance to this incident that explains why my collaborators chose to underline it? Is it possible to link it to the "Scroll on the Wall"? Does it further elucidate what it is like to be a young person in this particular setting, and does it help us to go from the particular to the general?

The space that Donald establishes for my collaborator is hypothetical, just as the space Stella created for him was. My collaborator resists both Stella and the nerds in this. The school reality of Donald and Richard differs from the school reality of my collaborator. They share the same physical space but not the same mental space. Later in the dialogue, my collaborator asks the nerds about the space they share.

COLLABORATOR: Okay, how do you feel about high school, being that this is your first year in high school . . . have you met any people yet?

RICHARD: I think the teachers and the staff are wonderful people.

COLLABORATOR: Of course, cuz you kiss ass.
[After this last remark, the dialogue deteriorated in that there was little communication and more insults. I thought my collaborator had gone from "cool," the preferred mode of inter-action, to anger.]

COLLABORATOR: You wanta snap, huh? Fine, where'd you get your socks from, huh? Army and Navy? Drippy Bo Diddley's? C'mon! All right! Who taught you how to match colors, Crayola Crayons?

My impressions were that the last few turns represent my collaborator's most agitated state in this dialogue. He obviously does not agree with Richard that teachers and staff are wonderful people. A space where the authorities are wonderful is not his space. What he says about going where life takes him, however, does not ring true when compared with other statements he makes. My collaborator talks about his prospects in six of the dialogues he engaged in. "Going where life takes me" is primarily a statement of his resistance to being put in other people's realities.

We might ask how such encounters affect the nerds. How many nerds, after experiencing such peer disparagement, give up being "good" students? Is trading in pocket protectors for gold chains enough to stop being a nerd, or do you have to forfeit your academic success as well? How many at-risk students started out as nerds? It might be interesting to find out how good students sustain themselves if they are surrounded by forceful peers who dislike school.

TEACHING IN THE OVERLAP

What Berger and Luckmann (1967) call "spheres of reality," Erickson (1986) calls "meaning systems." We have outlined how differences in the ways of life of less literate students and their teachers amounted to almost separate cultures. I would like to look at these mental representations as circles and consider how much overlap there is in the circles. One circle we will call "teacher reality" and the other "at-risk reality." It can only be in whatever shared reality there is that any education can take place.

Although the overlap we are talking about, if it exists, is a mental space, there is an actual physical space set aside for educational purposes. This, of course, is school. It might be the wrong place for the students we are concerned with, but it is real and not merely a mental representation. And if there is no shared mental space called school, there is no shared system of meaning in which teachers and students can function. The physical space called school would then be equivalent to a subway or a bus where a number of individuals happen to be riding together for any number of different reasons.

What are the commonalities of the groups? They share, for the most part, a common language and an everyday reality; most of our respondents could communicate in English, understand a money economy, and have some knowledge of the laws and rules of the larger society. They function socially together by means of fairly standardized role-relationships, but with highly differentiated roles. They each have a real need to be in the same physical space. Each group, however, has a different need and, although one could not function without the other, neither has a real payoff in meeting the other's need.

Why is each group in school? For teachers, school gives them their livelihood and their identity. If the teacher-self part of their identity is lessened, they become burned-out as long as they remain in school. They need students, but they don't need each student to succeed. High school teachers are regarded and most often regard themselves as teachers of subject matter rather than of students. If I give a well-prepared lecture on Shakespeare, I could say I taught English well that day, even if none of my students were paying attention.

The at-risk student needs to consolidate his selves into an identity. To do this he needs school to increase his literacy, to gain knowledge of the job market, and to link his skills and literacy to that job market. School, as it exists, is best equipped to help him increase his literacy, but less well equipped to carry out his other two significant needs. Increasing literacy is no small thing, but students, unfortunately, tend to hide their lack of literacy and avoid the tedious, and sometimes demeaning, work of gaining it, e.g. memorizing times tables, reading aloud from simplistic texts.

This concealment and avoidance seems to result from the institutionalized role-relationships that exist in school between at-risk students and their teachers. The grading system foists a judgmental role on teachers; students take tests or turn in work as directed, and teachers judge that work. It is natural that students should conceal or avoid that work which is judged inferior. Teachers may mean their judgments to be constructive, but students do not always share that meaning. Pointing out mistakes does not necessarily make for good teaching.

This is not to say that students are necessarily victims of autocratic teachers. Teachers often take on a role that has already been created for them. But they *are* authorities, at least in what they teach, and in an era when a principal feels he has to walk the corridors of his school with a baseball bat, no one wants to give up any authority that he might have. It may be that in most cases role-relationships cannot be changed because of institutionalization, fear of chaos, and simple inertia.

This leaves precious little overlap in which to teach. The two groups obviously share part of an everyday reality, but there may be no overlap whatsoever in the mental spaces of school that constitute part of their circles of reality. The fact that these young people are still hanging in as students implies that there is still a tenuous overarching universe that hints at a link between education and career. The problem is that, for them, even though education is essential, school is probably not the best place for it to occur.

This leads to the question of whether high schools can be reformed to educate the at-risk student. I do not believe this is possible unless we can reform the whole system, kindergarten through twelfth grade. Most of our respondents had too many educational handicaps to function in a traditional high school program. But even if we can eliminate many of the academic handicaps of our students, high school will still not be effective unless they can see a link between school and work. Such a link is obviously socially constructed, but it must be constructed by teachers and students alike. Students will not see the link unless their teachers do. It must exist in the overlap of their circles of reality, in the mental space as well as the physical space called school.

But even teachers often have a hard time finding direct links between what they teach and the world of work. As an English teacher, I dearly loved teaching John Milton's "L'Allegro" to college-bound students; both they and I saw the value of the poem. Understanding it, I thought, made one a better reader and a better thinker. In the next chapter I will describe another kind of teaching I dearly loved, where both my students and I saw an immediate payoff and a link between education and work. Not everyone can understand "L'Allegro," and the ability to understand it will not, in itself, make one a better person. What teachers have to do is find some way of showing a direct link between education and the future work of students. If they can do so with material they love to teach as much as I loved teaching "L'Allegro," they will be able to integrate *their* selves.

10
Learning in a Real-World Context

When considering the high school dropout problem, which is so huge that it gives the lie to the American notion of equal opportunity, I felt it imperative to give some kind of voice to the people most affected by the problem. The voices in the dialogues are mostly concerned with the pressures of competing selves. There were at least seven selves that contributed to the formation of an Eriksonian (Erikson, 1963) identity or, more simply, with finding the answer to the all-important question, "Where do I fit in?" These were self-as-my-work, sexual self, self-as-loyal-friend, self-in-peer-group, self-in-family, self-as-parent, and self-as-student.

School, unfortunately, has not been able to help many adolescents integrate these selves. Much of what goes on in classrooms is reported as "boring." However, even when class content is directed toward student interests, there is no guarantee that the class will be considered interesting. What makes a class boring seems to be how it is taught rather than what is taught. Sympathetic characteristics of teachers, although students could not specifically enumerate any, and teachers acting in a nonjudgmental manner are factors that contribute to interesting classes. There seems to be a relationship between pressure and boredom, as though students used boredom as a mechanism to defend themselves against school pressures.

There is a conflict between the "meaning systems" of students and those of teachers. Students are pressured by the attitudes of their peers, the demands of their impulses, the strictures of their families, their anxieties about their economic futures. School gives them, at most, a credential to deal with the economic world. Although teachers have their own but different pressures; for them, education has been the passport to relative economic security and, often, the basis of their identities. The teachers of at-risk students have been unable to convince those who drop out of school of the validity of education-based "meaning systems."

Recapitulating Erik Erikson's (1963) theories, we see that the adolescent tries to establish an identity by integrating her new social roles with what has gone before in her life. Successful integration, at this stage, is marked by the promise of a career; her identity crystallizes around a career direction. Teachers must be able to relate schooling to this quest for identity. If the world of school has little to do with the world of work, we cannot expect adolescents to want to attend. But content changes alone will not suffice; there must also be process changes.

CHANGING THE PROCESS OF SCHOOLING

Numbers of educators have created alternative programs within public school systems: remedial programs, schools within schools, alternative schools in separate sites, drop-in schools for those who have already dropped out. Characteristics of such programs include innovative subject matter, creative administrative structures, close supervision, student autonomy, frequent counseling, group dynamics. Many such programs have reported initial success; a few have been sustained.

The philosophies of such programs have varied greatly. The dropout program from which my collaborators were drawn has rigid attendance procedures, and a student's home is called in the morning if he is absent. Other programs seek to develop student autonomy by allowing as much freedom as possible. The ultimate extreme of the latter philosophy is what I will call education-as-group-therapy. The teachers in both types of program, no matter how much their philosophies diverge, are usually caring and dedicated people who have volunteered for that type of work. By taking one of the extremes, they deal with the autonomy vs. supervision tension that has befuddled high school teachers for years.

A brief look at three programs that I have been involved with demonstrates what has worked and what has not, and what kinds of education work in a dropout-prevention program. Following the method of this book, we seek our data in particular places. How far we can go from the particular to the general is arguable, but by dealing with a particular setting we may be able to answer one of Frederick Erickson's (1986) original questions: "How is it that it can make sense to students to learn in one situation and not in another?"

An Alternative High School

In 1971, with the aid of federal funds then earmarked for innovative programs, I was able to set up an alternative high school with its own facility in the Rutland, Vermont public school system. Students officially earned their credits from their sending high schools, but took most, if not all, their work with us. Our population was made up of disaffected students or those interested in having more autonomy over their learning. In those days of free-flowing federal money and the school reform atmosphere of the 1960s, we thought that freedom was the answer to all problems in education.

I served as director of the school and full-time teacher. Seventy students were enrolled in the program. We had one other full-time teacher; one full-time aide with a college degree (who became a de facto teacher); one three-day-a-week teacher; and a part-time aide with excellent tool knowledge and resourcefulness, who also functioned as a teacher. All were enthusiastic and dedicated. We contracted with an unaccredited private school to teach two field-oriented science courses for us. Instead of paying the school, we agreed to enroll a number of their students in our program so they could earn credits. With such a staffing arrangement and a relatively inexpensive rent for our building, we had the lowest per-pupil expenditure among all the state's high schools.

Before the school opened we had group meetings with prospective students to find out what course work they wanted. We set up a mini-course system with a new registration every three weeks, instituted modular scheduling, and set aside one morning a week for whole group convocations on a town-meeting format. By state law, school attendance was mandatory, but we made class attendance voluntary. It was the job of the teachers, we decided, to make the classes interesting enough to ensure students coming.

By the middle of October, the part-time biology teacher approached me with much enthusiasm, wanting my approval to "wrap up" biology in another two weeks. I reminded him that the course was state-mandated, and that a number of students needed a laboratory science on their transcript for college admission. But he had had a few exciting classes talking about student concerns, he argued, and he

wanted to spend the rest of the year doing "group therapy." That was
far more important than biology, he assured me. Never mind that he
had absolutely no training in group therapy; never mind that he was a
gifted teacher who had an undergraduate major in biology and a
master of arts in teaching; never mind that it was precisely his training
in biology and teaching that was enabling him to make a living. I
insisted on a biology course; the ensuing tension between autonomy
and supervision was to split the staff for the rest of that year.

In spite of conservative opposition in the town, student clashes
with the administration of the sending schools, and a few irresponsible
teachers, the school continued for three years. The districts chose not
to continue the program when federal funds had run out. Only four
students had dropped out, and only from personal pressures that no
school could overcome. No one dropped out because of boredom.
Although we were interested in alternative education rather than
school attrition, what we had was a very cost-effective dropout-prevention program.

As an educational endeavor, however, we had failed. The minority who had wanted to go to college went. None of the others had any
marketable skills, nor did they have any clear sense of where they fit
in. I doubt, however, if they would have done any better in the
traditional program, and the specter of the military draft during the
school's first year enabled, if not caused, the young men in the school
to postpone any decision making on careers. More unfortunate,
though, they did not seem to have developed a sense of responsibility
or a work ethic of any kind.

At one point I was teaching a course in psychology. The students
had suggested such a course, attracted by popular notions of the subject.
One day I was teaching psychoanalytic theory. I thought it was one of
those days where the atmosphere was electric. The interactions were
stimulating to everyone: It seemed that they were internalizing the
theory and applying it to their own lives as well as learning it. After the
class I was both exhilarated and exhausted. In my seven years of teaching up till then, it was perhaps the best single class I had experienced.

The next day two of twenty students showed up. I was disappointed, but assumed I had exaggerated what I had felt and that the
class had not been very interesting after all. Later that day, I saw one
of the students who had been absent and asked how he had liked the
previous day's class. With much enthusiasm, he said it was the best
class he had ever had and that everybody had loved it. I then asked
him why he did not come that morning. He casually replied that most
of the kids had spent the day at Airport Lookout drinking wine.

Airport Lookout is a beautiful location on the Long Trail that overlooks the entire valley that contains Rutland, Vermont. It gives a wonderful view of the Green and the Taconic Mountains and, much as I enjoy teaching psychology, I would probably prefer, on almost any warm sunny day, to spend the time there drinking wine with my friends. But, although I felt a responsibility to teach the class, I had not developed any similar sense of responsibility among the students to attend the class. It made more sense to them to spend the day elsewhere. Were I an employer, I would not be interested in hiring any of those people.

They had remained in high school; they had even enjoyed high school. But it had no connection to the world of work. Neither was I led to believe that any of their discussions on the mountain or their group therapies contributed much to the understanding of themselves. After all, they knew they could have gone to Airport Lookout on Saturday but could only learn psychology on the weekdays. Our reluctance to make demands on them allowed their decisions to be made on impulse. They did not have nightmares of ending up as street beggars; their setting insulated them. We could create such a school for Michael and perhaps prevent his dropping out, but we would not be serving him well.

An Apprenticeship Program

Years later, in the small town of Falmouth, Maine, a number of young people were better served in a program that placed them in jobs in that town and in a nearby small city. At that time I was a special education teacher on the secondary level, and we needed a program that would go beyond teaching students basic academic skills. Academic skills may help a student be more successful in school, but they guarantee no success in life. No one was more aware of this than the students, who were always complaining about course work, asking, "What does this have to do with any kind of job?"

So one year we decided to get them jobs. Many colleges offered cooperative education programs, where students earn money while going to school. Although our students did not have sufficient job skills, our director of special education scoured the area for apprenticeships. We wanted placements for students where they would work several hours a day without pay provided that the "employer" teach them how to do a specific job.

The notion of apprenticeship is nothing new. At one time in our history it was the primary way young men learned job skills. Compulsory education, child labor laws, and growth of labor unions eroded the practice. Although these were progressive reforms, we may have thrown the baby out with the bathwater. A self-taught friend of mine established a highly successful sign-painting business and looked in vain for years for an apprentice to whom he could teach the business and then sell it to when he retired. While I was studying for my doctorate in 1985, he even offered me the chance.

How prevalent are such opportunities? More, apparently, than many people believe. In our program we placed a student, Mike, in a body shop, although the employer had not planned to take on any new employees. The employer, of course, was getting some free labor, but he could have gotten along quite well without Mike. The big payoff for the body shop turned out to be in teaching a young person. The other employees did not feel threatened by Mike and felt better about themselves because they were teaching somebody something. In my experience, I never learned anything so well as when I taught it.

We were able to place several young women in a day-care center. One's attendance record was too poor for her to learn anything or to make a contribution to the center, and she was eventually removed. Another, however, did very well. She found work that she could do and her self-confidence increased. Parents of young women, as was expected, were less reluctant to agree to allow their daughters to work outside school than were parents of young men. Opposition, we thought, would be overcome as the program became better known.

If we could erase our Dickensian image of exploited apprentices, such programs might have enormous potential if monitored. What we decided that ours lacked was the building of a cohort and a holding environment where a qualified adult could be available to refer students to services. Our students returned to school and attended regular classes or did work in the school resource room. Being isolated from their peers on the job they did not have the advantage of having friends close at hand.

The Gang of Four

With what we learned from the apprenticeship program, we set up something different the following year. Four young men were well served, not by good times or group therapy, but by learning in a real-world context set within a holding environment. As part of my job I was often asked to deal with students considered to be behavior problems. In the year in question we had four over-age ninth graders who had no interest in school. I had previously taught them, but with

little success. They had problems at home, used drugs, occasionally
had minor scrapes with the law, such as shoplifting, and were disruptive in class. One had been diagnosed as learning disabled, and another
as a slow learner. Two had been retained in grade. Whereas the
majority of that school's population were middle-class and college-bound, the Gang of Four, as we named them, stood out and were
unwelcome by most teachers. Neither were we willing to recommend
them to an employer.

The school district was part of a consortium that could send
juniors and seniors to an excellent area vocational school, the graduates
of which almost always found jobs in their area of specialization. But,
as ninth graders, the Gang of Four were not eligible for that program.
Moreover, the young man who was a slow learner did not have an
interest in developing the small motor skills necessary to master most
crafts. The already skilled mechanic of the group was learning disabled and had little patience with the reading that is required in
vocational programs.

It is said that special education teachers have the highest burnout
rate in the profession. It was my seventeenth year in teaching and my
fifth in special education, and I was a full-fledged case. The last place I
wanted to be every day was in school. On opening day I was approached by Connie Goldman, the junior high school administrator;
and Emily Taylor, the coordinator of special education. They wondered *what* we were going to do with the Gang of Four during their
last year in junior high. On a whim, I told them I would be willing to
assume all responsibility for their education. I would teach them how
to build a house, and I would make sure that, in the process, they
earned and were credited with all the language arts, social studies,
science, mathematics that they would ordinarily be expected to cover
in their regular classes. Not only that, but I would see to it that they
were out of the school building from the time the bus arrived in the
morning until it left in the afternoon.

I did not believe they would take me up on my offer, but Connie
asked me to give her a written description. The next day they showed
it to Ted Sharp, the junior–senior high school principal. Connie, Ted,
and Emily are three of the best educators I have ever worked with.
There were times when we fought, when I was angry at one or more
of them, when I filed grievances. An angry exchange of letters we
had may still be on file. But we never lost respect for each other and
they remain my friends. Not only did they approve my project but
they agreed to pay mileage when I transported the Gang of Four in
my car.

As it happened, I owned some acreage and had recently taken a course in how to build an energy-efficient house. I offered the Gang of Four "jobs." In exchange for credits, getting out of the school building each day, and learning how to build a house, they would give me four to five hours a day of hard physical labor, keep a daily journal, and follow my directions. After a few minutes of disbelief, they enthusiastically agreed. For the rest of the year I met them each day at the school bus; if anyone was absent, we would drive to his house to find out why.

The fact that it was *my* house meant I would get the benefits of their labor. At the time, with 48 hours to begin a program, we had no other choice. The Gang of Four and their parents were aware of the situation and gave their permission. If I had had money or had there been other funds available, they would have been paid a wage just as my collaborators were in the project that led to this book.

Until the first snowfall of that year in late December, the Gang of Four and I purchased tools and materials, cleared land, felled trees, made a road, ditched it, built a culvert to drain it, dealt with local government authorities for necessary permits, hand-dug a foundation, laid out a house, poured concrete, set and leveled posts, bolted on sills, calculated how thick our floor joists had to be to span the width of the house, dealt with a local sawmill and learned the ins and outs of the lumber business.

When the weather was inclement we would drive to a shopping mall, and I would give them such problems as how to spend an imaginary $100 on the tools they considered necessary to build a house. Each one had to come back with an individual list, which we would then compare with the others. They learned a great deal about tools, and by the time it snowed we had used those tools to get a house above the ground.

During the winter we tried to learn more about the environment, but more time was spent indoors. In one of the school shops we prefabricated an ice-fishing house that we tried to transport, piece by piece, on the roof of my VW Bug to a nearby pond. We did not succeed. In the spring, because of depleted construction funds, we stayed closer to school. We added two young women to our group and took water samples from a brook that we believed was contaminated by the school's septic system. In addition, we took photographs of the effluent for the school board. The system was ordered to be repaired.

The Gang of Four learned English by keeping their daily journals and by reading well-illustrated construction manuals. In addition, they tried to make sense out of local building codes and environmental regulations. Each filled out one of the many permits we had to have, even to burn refuse. On one rainy day we went to the public library, and I showed them how to find their way around the reference section; we used the texts to learn how deep the frost level was in our latitude so we would know how deep to set the footings for our foundation. They spoke with town officials and merchants. We spoke with one another.

Social studies was, of course, local government. A court appearance that two of the Gang of Four were required to make made for some discussion. Why there were so many regulations made for more. We talked with my neighbors to feel them out on whether they would object if I applied for a building variance. Whether people had the right to post their land was hotly disputed. The Gang of Four could not list the president's cabinet, but they learned who the governor was when he proposed a bill to the legislature that regulated snowmobiling.

Environmental science and geology were the subject matter of that part of the curriculum. A wooded acre will yield a cord of firewood a year without depleting the forest. The percolation ability of our sandy loam called for a $20' \times 70'$ leachbed. Where water is likely to flow down a hill and where bedrock was were things to be discovered. We found out where the deer drank and where mosquitoes were likely to breed. Sumac tea washed down our lunch one—and only one—day.

When I showed them the formulas to calculate beam span, they learned to plug in the variables for kind of wood, distance on center, and spanning distance. They were surprised afterwards when I told them they were doing algebra. How could they be sure, I asked, that the plot we staked out for the house was a perfect rectangle? They believed me when I told them to make the diagonals equal and said they understood when I proved it with geometry. (They *did* learn to use the Pythagorean theorem.)

Their transcripts at the end of that year listed English, general mathematics, government, environmental science, industrial arts, and physical education as courses that totaled 5¼ of the 16 credits needed for graduation. The Gang of Four had earned as many credits as anyone else and thoroughly enjoyed returning to school in the afternoons covered with dirt and mud, evidence that they had accomplished something that their peers had not.

They had spent their days doing what they considered to be "real" work. Even though they were achieving academically, other students and some teachers still looked askance at them. We all stood out when we were in the school building (Were we in the wrong place?) On one occasion, however, because people were used to us being filthy, we yielded to convention and spent one day in the school building drawing attention to ourselves by being jacketed and tied in our Sunday best.

And without substituting "group therapy" or whatever for subject matter, other things happened to us. When you do such work as cutting down trees, you come to depend on your fellow workers. I can make a tree fall in a planned direction 9 of 10 times; a professional can do it 99 out of 100 times. But there is always that time when a strong wind, a peculiar grain of wood, or a miscalculation can make things very dangerous, and when you are close to the tree you may not be able to hear the crack of the wood over the noise of your chainsaw. Your companions' shouts and signals tell you to get out of the way. We had to depend on each other for our lives.

The slow learner was fearless when it came to climbing trees or walking up the incline of a tree kept from falling by the branches of another so he could trim it and let it settle to the ground. But we always made sure one of us held the end of a rope that was around his waist and hooked over the branch of a standing tree. (All the while we assured him that we did not care if he broke his head but the forms to be filled out if he did and the school's insurance company investigators would be too much of a hassle.)

One day when each of the Gang of Four was in a four-foot hole he was digging for a foundation post, I decided to take some photographs for Connie, Emily, and Ted to show to the school board. I called the name of one of the gang who had not seen me set the focus; when he looked up into my twin lens reflex, he remarked that his mother had had a camera like that. For some reason, perhaps because of the tone of his voice, the other three stopped working and climbed out of their holes. He related to us that his mother had committed suicide a few years before or, at least, that they were pretty sure it was suicide, and he told us details of her body being found in Casco Bay. Only the slow learner gave a verbal reaction, which was something like, "Gee, that must have been tough." In a while we all went back to work.

Sometime later I mentioned this to the father of the young man who told of his mother's death. We were acquainted and he told me that, as far as he knew, that was the first time his son had talked of his mother's suicide. He had not been aware that the young man even accepted that it was a suicide. Apparently, a secure-enough environment had evolved for such things to be mentioned. We trusted each other and collaborated to create a "meaning system."

We had created a "meaning system" in which it made sense for the Gang of Four to learn and me to teach. It made sense because we were in a real-world environment. They were learning to use the tools of their technology, from hammers to libraries, and they could see a direct relation between those tools and their lives. We saw the results of our labor each day and viewed our finished products. We had real-world accomplishments, and each of us was confident he would be able to build a house should he choose to. And education reasserted itself in my life as a meaningful endeavor.

The success of this or similar projects and the group unity depended on the *work*. I could have taught a course in construction, but if there were not a real house to build, the course would have been only an abstraction. If students could not hold the tools in their hands, they might not have bothered to learn about them. The *work* of building the house gave us a core to expand from. A course in construction might teach some how to *conceptualize* building houses, but the Gang of Four needed to *build* one (or part of one) house. They needed to go from the particular to the general.

THE REAL WORLD OF EDUCATION

Programs like building a house with the Gang of Four can be replicated elsewhere. The essential parts of such a program are (1) the teacher, (2) the work, (3) students who agree to perform tasks in return for something they value, and (4) a school system that grants autonomy to teachers. *One* teacher must have total responsibility for the formal education of his students. The students should be able to choose their work and teacher. There must be *one* core of work that both the teacher and students value and that is valued, in monetary as well as in aesthetic or moral terms, by the greater society. There must be something to be completed and that students could learn as they are doing it. The project cannot be seen by students simply as a means of creating a secure environment for them; that system proved a failure at the Alternative School. Students must have roles to play in the project and agree to specific responsibilities. Both the teachers and the students must have something to gain.

Lauren Resnick (1975, 1987) has suggested that learning needed for school success differs from that needed for job success. As a cognitive psychologist, she is also concerned with the development of thinking skills. In particular, she identifies abstract thinking and the ability to step out of a system and reason about it as skills necessary for survival. She calls for apprenticeship-type programs that encourage:

1. socially shared intellectual work, built around mutual accomplishment of tasks, so that elements of the skill take on meaning within a wider context
2. observation and student comment as skills are built up while making processes of thinking visible
3. organization around particular bodies of knowledge rather than around general abilities.

The curriculum for the Gang of Four was organized around a particular body of knowledge. Digging a hole may not seem to be very intellectual, but digging it to a depth below the known frost line makes it intellectual work. Moreover, it is work within a context, that is, building a house. The work was socially shared and previously hidden processes, such as laying out a house square, calculating the dimension of a beam relative to its span, became overt.

What the Gang of Four was engaged in was not simply training for a particular job. Nor should that be the sole object of similar programs. Resnick (1975, 1987) believes that school should concentrate on preparing young people to be good adaptive learners so they can perform competently in unpredictable situations. The Gang of Four learned the process of building a house from the ground up; presumably, their skills can be transferred to other processes.

The slow learner of the gang never managed to learn such skills as the complete times tables. Building a house did not teach him that, but neither had nine years of previous schooling. He did, however, have a pocket calculator that served his needs. He was also offered a real-world job. The sawmill operator we dealt with saw in him a willing worker, capable of learning, and offered him an apprenticeship-job during which he would learn the business. I did not necessarily expect the Gang of Four to go into construction; I did expect them to see learning as meaningful and to increase their employability.

I also expected that the Gang of Four would increase the amounts of literacy available to them. David Harman (1986) believes that people learn to read when being literate is in their self-interest. I think this principle extends to all kinds of literacy. Harman gives the example of 42 men who wanted to be certified as exterminators but who were not able to read the licensing examination. Their union taught them to read the actual training manuals for exterminators, as the Gang of Four read construction manuals, and all 42 passed the test. When the

Pythagorean theorem was perceived as necessary to design a house, the Gang of Four (with the slow learner using his calculator) learned it.

Would such programs be possible in urban as well as rural environments? The Gang of Four lived in a suburban environment, but did their work in a rural one. There are, of course, many arguments why such programs would not work in cities and towns. The city is not physically conducive to such projects. Even if we were able and willing to take on such projects, they would not be cost-effective. The bureaucratic problems alone to get the necessary permissions would be insurmountable. You cannot have "gangs" out of school and running around a city. The possibility of abuse is rampant; didn't I exploit the situation to get free labor to build *my* house?

I would argue, however, that the city is the environment *most* conducive to these types of projects. There is more to do in the city; that is why people choose to live in them. City students have the advantage of public transportation, which the Gang of Four did not have. The city may not be the place to build a single-family house, but it might well be the place to renovate an apartment, shoot an ethnographic film, open a car-repair shop, start a luncheonette, institute a mail service, establish a theatre group, set up a food co-op, build a playground, publish a newspaper, run a day-care center, create a job bank, and a young people's employment service.

With one teacher for the Gang of Four, it could be argued that the project was not cost-effective. The fact that each of the gang was classified as a student needing special services allowed us to spend more than the average. The district was reimbursed by the state for most of my salary. But what restricted me to only four students, more than anything else, was the size of my car. I would propose a one-to-eight teacher–student ratio on projects like those listed above. One-to-eight, incidentally, has been the ratio for the basic unit in the American army, the squad, for many years; while we are not interested in a militaristic orientation, there is evidence that such a ratio makes for effective supervision. A larger group than that would be unwieldy. This ratio brings the per-pupil cost down; nevertheless, even if the cost remains high, the consequences of a 40 percent dropout rate on unemployment, homelessness, and the social services they require would eventually be higher.

Such a program would depend on willing and able teachers. I believe they are there now, and others could be trained. There are already people within the public school systems who have established alternative programs, or who realize that the current system is not working and yearn to do something different. There are teachers who leave the profession because they feel they have no autonomy in deciding what to teach and where to teach it. Connie, Emily, and Ted were willing to grant me that autonomy. They believed me when I said I would be responsible for the education for the Gang of Four.

The most significant reform in setting up such projects is not that there will be structural change; the Gang of Four remained within the public school administrative, though not physical, structure. It is not even that there will be numbers of students outside of classrooms; that happens now. The most significant change is in the concept of what a teacher is. A teacher must be a co-creator, with the students, of a meaning system or a reality. And that reality must overlap with the reality of the larger society.

The teacher in such a program must have considerably more autonomy than most teachers now have. She must have the autonomy to create a curriculum and to determine what credits a student has earned. Moreover, she must be the kind of person who is willing to take the responsibility for the education of her students. She must be co-worker, teacher, counselor, and authority figure.

To anyone mired in an overly bureaucratic system, this still may seem to be a pie-in-the-sky notion. I suggest that now, when the dropout problem is perceived as so momentous, is the most opportune time to institute such programs. Administrators and political figures in their current dire circumstances will be more open to experimental projects. Schools may have less control over students in these programs, but students might feel more accountable to their group. Surely this proposal will not make for *more* dropouts than we have now.

That such a project worked once with the Gang of Four means there is a good possibility that it could work again with other students in another setting. The data on which this book is based have shown that many students are pressured by parental and societal values on one side and their own impulses on the other. School has not shown them that they have a place in the larger society that attempts to impose values on them. To many, yielding to their impulses and to the values of the streets offer a greater promise. All the data point to their need to find a place where it will make sense to learn the tools of their technology, and where they will see both an immediate and an ultimate payoff for their work. I do not believe our society can tolerate the problem of inadequately trained people who are denied the pursuit of happiness. If what has been proposed appears too fraught with problems, consider the alternative. The present system is not working for substantial numbers of our youth. If there are both teachers and students who want to engage in such programs, what have we got to lose? This book tried to analyze the lives of people who were in the wrong place at the wrong time. We can neither change who the people are nor how old they are. We can, however, change the nature of the places they find themselves in.

References
Index
About the Author

References

Berger, P., and Luckmann, T. (1967). *The social construction of reality: A treatise on the sociology of knowledge.* New York: Doubleday.

Billingsly, A. (1987). *The state of Black America.* Washington, DC: National Urban League.

Bruner, J. (1986). *Actual minds, possible worlds.* Cambridge, MA: Harvard University Press.

Children's Defense Fund. (1988). *A children's reform budget: FY 1988.* Washington, DC: Author.

Covington, M., & Beery, R. (1976). *Self worth and school learning.* New York: Holt, Rinehart & Winston.

Erickson, F. (1976). Gatekeeping encounter: A social selection process. In P. Sanday (Ed.), *Anthropology and the public interest* (pp. 111–145). New York: Academic Press.

Erickson, F. (1986). Qualitative methods in research on teaching. In M. C. Whitrock (Ed.), *Handbook of research in teaching* (3rd ed., pp. 119–161). New York: Macmillan.

Erikson, E. (1963). *Childhood and society.* New York: Norton.

Farrell, E., Peguero, G., Lindsey, R., & White, R. (1988). Giving voice to high school students: Pressure and boredom, ya know what I'm sayin'? *American Educational Research Journal, 25,* 489–502.

Fine, M. (1985). Dropping out of high school: An inside look. *Social Policy, 16* (2), 43–50.

Fine, M. (1986). Why urban adolescents drop out of public high school. *Teachers College Record, 87,* 393–409.

Fine, M. (1987). Silencing in public schools. *Language Arts, 64,* 157–174.

Fine, M. (1988). Sexuality, schooling, and adolescent females: The missing discourse of desire. *Harvard Educational Review, 58,* 29–53.

Gardner, H. (1983). *Frames of mind: The theory of multiple intelligences.* New York: Basic Books.

Gilligan, C. (1982). *In a different voice: Psychological theory and woman's development.* Cambridge, MA: Harvard University Press.

167

Gould, S. (1981). *The mismeasure of man.* New York: Norton.

Harman, D. (1986). *Illiteracy: A national dilemma.* New York: Cambridge Book.

Ingram, L. (1988). Case study: JHS 143. Unpublished paper. The City College, City University of New York.

Jensen, A. (1969). How much can we boost I.Q. and scholastic achievement. *Harvard Educational Review.* Reprint Series No. 2:1–123.

Jensen, A. (1973). *Educability and group differences.* New York: Harper.

Kohlberg, L. (1981). *The philosophy of moral development.* San Francisco: Harper and Row.

Lee, V., & Ekstrom, R. (1987). Student access to guidance counseling in high school. *American Educational Research Journal, 24,* 287–310.

Lewin, T. (1988, March 20). Fewer teen mothers, but more are unmarried. *New York Times,* p. 6.

Malinowski, B. (1961). *Argonauts of the western Pacific.* New York: E. P. Dutton.

Mead, G. (1934). *Mind, self, and society.* Chicago: University of Chicago Press.

Mead, M. (1941). *From the South Seas: Studies of adolescence and sex in primitive societies.* New York: William Morrow. (Original work published 1928)

Mead, M. (1961). *Coming of age in Samoa: A psychological study of primitive youth for Western civilization.* New York: William Morrow. (Original work published 1928)

Moynihan, D. (1989, January 29). Yes, we do need a "methadone clone." *New York Times,* p. 25.

Nance, J. (1975). *The gentle Tasaday: A stone age people in the Philippine rain forest.* New York: Harcourt Brace.

Ogbu, J. (1978). *Minority education and caste: The American system in cross-cultural perspective.* Orlando, FL: Academic Press.

Opie, I., & Opie, P. (1959). *The lore and language of the school child.* Oxford: Clarendon.

Orr, E. (1987). *Twice as less: Black English and the performance of Black students in mathematics and science.* New York: Norton.

Piaget, J., & Inhelder, B. (1969). *The psychology of the child.* New York: Basic Books.

Powell, A., Farrar, E., & Cohen, D. (1985). *The shopping mall high school: Winners and losers in the educational marketplace.* Boston: Houghton Mifflin.

Read, E. (1988, March 17). Birth cycle: For poor teen-agers, pregnancies become new rite of passage. *The Wall Street Journal,* p. 1.

Resnick, L. (1975). *Adaptive education for young children.* Manhattan, KS: Learning Resource Development.

Resnick, L. (1987). *Education and learning to think.* Washington, DC: National Academy Press.

Seager, J., & Olson, A. (1986). *Women in the world: An international atlas*.
New York: Simon and Schuster.

Selman, R., & Glidden, M. (1987, Fall). Negotiation strategies for youth.
School Safety, pp. 18–21.

Smith, F. (1989). Overselling literacy. *Phi Delta Kappan, 70*, 352–359.

Sullivan, H. (1953). *The interpersonal theory of psychiatry*. New York: Norton.

Wilson, W. (1987). *The truly disadvantaged: The inner city, the underclass,
and public policy*. Chicago: University of Chicago Press.

Winnicott, D. (1971). *Therapeutic consultations in child psychiatry*. New York:
Basic Books.

Index

About the Author

Edwin Farrell is an Associate Professor in the Department of Social and Psychological Foundations at the City College in New York. In 1985, he received his Ed.D. from the Laboratory for Human Development at Harvard University. He was a teacher in public and private schools in New York, New Jersey, Vermont, and Maine from 1963 to 1983 and served in the Vermont State Legislature from 1972 to 1974. He founded and directed an alternative high school, and has taught students of all ages and levels of ability.